I0842692

TWO EMANCIPATIONS, ONE MORE TO GO

Releasing the Black Mind from the Shackles of Oppression

Reginald F. Davis, Ph.D.

an imprint of Sunbury Press, Inc.
Mechanicsburg, PA USA

an imprint of Sunbury Press, Inc.
Mechanicsburg, PA USA

Copyright © 2026 by Reginald F. Davis.
Cover Copyright © 2026 by Sunbury Press, Inc.

Sunbury Press supports copyright. Copyright fuels creativity, encourages diverse voices, promotes free speech, and creates a vibrant culture. Thank you for buying an authorized edition of this book and for complying with copyright laws by not reproducing, scanning, or distributing any part of it in any form without permission. You are supporting writers and allowing Sunbury Press to continue to publish books for every reader. For information contact Sunbury Press, Inc., Subsidiary Rights Dept., PO Box 548, Boiling Springs, PA 17007 USA or legal@sunburypress.com.

For information about special discounts for bulk purchases, please contact Sunbury Press Orders Dept. at (855) 338-8359 or orders@sunburypress.com.

To request one of our authors for speaking engagements or book signings, please contact Sunbury Press Publicity Dept. at publicity@sunburypress.com.

FIRST SCRIPTORIA PRESS EDITION: February 2026

Set in Adobe Garamond | Interior design by Crystal Devine | Cover by Lawrence Knorr | Edited by Lawrence Knorr.

Publisher's Cataloging-in-Publication Data
Names: Davis, Reginald F., author.
Title: Two emancipations : releasing the Black mind from the shackles of oppression / Reginald F. Davis, Ph.D.
Description: First trade paperback edition. | Mechanicsburg, PA : Scriptoria Press, 2026.
Summary: Black people have an opportunity in this 21st Century to become a
people of socioeconomic power needed to control their own institutions and destiny. They have undergone two emancipations and have one more to go which is the decolonization of their minds to create a different reality in the future than they have had in the past. No one can do this for black Americans; they must do this for themselves. There is no doubt they have the power within their collective hands to cancel their captivity. To cancel their captivity, their minds must undergo mental emancipation to break from the shackles of their oppression.
Identifiers: ISBN 979-8-88819-427-0 (softcover).
Subjects: RELIGION / Christian Education / Children & Youth | RELIGION / Christian Ministry / Youth | SELF-HELP / General.

Designed in the USA
0 1 1 2 3 5 8 13 21 34 55

For the Love of Books!

This is dedicated to Black Americans and
black people of the diaspora.

We know that there are many things wrong in the white world, but there are many things wrong in the black world, too. We can't keep on blaming the white man. There are things we must do for ourselves.

—Martin Luther King, Jr.

CONTENTS

ACKNOWLEDGMENTS

I want to thank my wife Myrlene for her support; my daughter Nandi for the subtitle of the book; Joel for his suggestions, and the rest of the Davis family for their prayers and support. I also thank Dr. Lawrence Knorr and the Sunbury Press team for accepting this work for publication. Their professionalism is invaluable.

INTRODUCTION

There is no gainsaying that black people have been torn apart by racism, terrorism, and oppression. Black people's bodies, minds, emotions, and spirits have been ripped apart, and it is up to them to bring together the torn pieces of their lives to be whole. W.E.B. Dubois called this balkanization "Double consciousness . . . an American, a Negro; two souls, two thoughts, two unreconciled strivings; two warring ideals in one dark body, whose dogged strength alone keeps it from being torn asunder."[1] The struggle to bring together what has been torn apart has been long and arduous. Black people wonder when the dawn of justice, equality, and total liberation will come for them. Although Black people have been waiting for the dawn of justice and liberation, they have made some progress on their American journey.

With two hundred and fifty years of slavery, one hundred years of segregation and exploitation, and fifty-five years ago, black people gained their civil and voting rights. This shows their struggle has not been in vain, even though much of civil rights is gutted; affirmative action has ended, diversity, equity, and inclusion eliminated, black history sanitized, books banned, 300,000 black women lost their government jobs, black unemployment is high again, and a lot of black history taken out of black museums, black people must turn to themselves because they hold the solution to much of their collective problems. The Black Lives Matter movement has lost most of its luster but still continues to focus on self determination and liberation in local communities. Having been blocked socially, educationally, economically, and politically for many centuries, and victims of ongoing broken promises, blacks are still struggling to make America

---

1. W.E.B. Dubois, *The Souls of Black Folk* (New York: Penguin, 1969), 45–46.

deliver on its Constitutional promise of life, liberty, and the pursuit of happiness. There is no gainsaying, "Had the Lord not been on their side," black people would have perished during their American experience. It is a truism that black people are truly a strong and resilient people. Their oppressors could not drown them out, lynch them out, genocide them out, despair them out, and put them out of this nation where their sweat, tears, and blood have cemented their stay in this land called "The home of the brave, the land of the free." It is an understatement that black people have gone through hell in America, and are still going through it with all the injustice, inequality, gerrymandering, gentrification, and outright erasing of black contributions to this nation.

No other racial group has gone through what black Americans have experienced. The words of the Apostle Paul can truly be applied to them. "We are troubled on every side, yet not distressed; we are perplexed, but not in despair; persecuted, but not forsaken; cast down, but not destroyed" (2 Corinthians 4:8-9). Because black people's resilience was stronger than oppression, racism, hate, lies, evil, injustice, despair, lynch mobs, terrorism, biting dogs, water hoses, and prison cells, it is a testament that God is with black people, and God is not finished with them yet. Although they are wandering in this American wilderness, not knowing which way to go, God is not finished with black people. They have contributed much to this land and received so little. They have built America's buildings, bridges, economic floor, and fought in every American war to help this nation promote the ideas of freedom and democracy when justice, equality, and fairness have been denied to them. They have done so many great things in this nation that one cannot tell them all. The great investment of black people in the progress of this nation and the nil to no return on their investment is America's shame. Carol Anderson said, "Millions of enslaved people and their ancestors had built the enormous wealth of the United States; indeed, in 1860, 80 percent of the nation's gross national product was tied to slavery. Yet, in return for nearly 250 years of toil, African Americans had received nothing but rape, whippings, murder, the dismemberment of families, and forced subjugation, illiteracy, and abject poverty."[2]

---

2. Carol Anderson, *White Rage The Unspoken Truth of Our Racial Divide*, (New York: Bloomsbury Publisher, 2017), 11.

Despite US treatment, black people are some of the most loyal, patriotic, loving, and forgiving people in America. What else can explain why they have not turned on their oppressors? What else can explain why they have not become an ISIS terrorist group? Martin Luther King, Jr. was amazed that out of all the evil, injustice, grief, and inhumanity America has inflicted and still inflicts on black people, they have not turned on their oppressors nor on the idea of justice, democracy, and humanity. What else can be shown to demonstrate that black people love America, too? Black people have shown over and over and over again that they are not America's enemy. Yet, after 406 years, black people are still plagued by powerlessness, white racism and police terrorism. They are still the victims of an unjust system that is protected and promoted against them. Unless it is otherwise proven, America will not change its modus operandi towards black people, but black people must change the way they think of themselves and develop the power to counter those forces against them. America is a morally and spiritually sick nation in need of the Great Physician, who is Jesus Christ. Martin Luther King, Jr. acknowledged the sickness in his last speech in Memphis in 1968. He talked about how there were threats on his life, "By some of our sick white brothers." This sickness, the next day, took King's life.

The sickness of white supremacy and racism still affects black people to the point that many of them turn on themselves instead of to themselves. When the air is filled with toxic gases of racism, it does affect the people who are trying to protect themselves from it. Black Americans have struggled hard to clear the air of this toxic gas, but many have succumbed to it. Unless black people come together and put on a breathing apparatus of self-sufficiency to stop the toxic air of damning ideas, beliefs, and values from getting into the far reaches of their inner selves that produce self-hatred, coming out of the pandemic of their long oppression is prolonged mistrust and disunity. They must concentrate on healing themselves first and foremost. Since America is rejecting justice for black people in its socio-economic political life and policies, and since the roll back of their progress in terms of civil rights, voting, government contracts, and the bad check that America has given black people of which Martin Luther King, Jr. talked about in his "I have a Dream" speech keeps bouncing, what are black people to do in this 21 century while living in this American Empire? Where do they go from here? The answer is they must turn to themselves because no one is coming to save nor liberate them. They must do this for themselves, and practice group dynamics like other racial groups. They must concentrate on building and acquiring power to achieve socioeconomic independence! Booker T. Washington said, "At the bottom of education, at the bottom of politics, even at the bottom of religion, there must be for our race economic independence." This isolated independence is not the goal but a necessary strategy to help black people heal psychologically, spiritually, socially, and economically, eventually becoming part of an interdependence that respects them. Without social, economic, and political power, black people will not be respected nor able to stop the oppressive forces against them.

Amos Wilson said, "The White Man oppresses Afrikan peoples because he possesses the power to do so. The Black Man is oppressed because he has not developed the power to prevent his oppression. His oppression will end when the power of his oppressor is countered by his own power."[3] Without economic and social power, black people cannot liberate themselves from the white power structure. The issue is power. Oppression is driven by economics and power. The reason black people could not stop the African holocaust is that they had no power; the reason they could not stop institutional slavery, they had no power; the reason they could not stop Jim Crow, they had no power. What is happening to black people today is the result of having no power. Black people, at least in America, are a praying people, but they need power. They are churchgoing people, but they need power. They are a marching people, but they need power. Only power respects power, and until black people harness socioeconomic and political power, they won't be able to counter the power against them.

It will take some time for black people to gain power equal to white power because of centuries of denying black people human rights and unfair socioeconomic policies that serve the interests of the elite. However, black people must start pooling their resources—nearly 2 trillion dollars— to create four essential institutions that will set the trend upward. They need their own banks to give loans to start black businesses; they need

---

3. Amos Wilson, *Blueprint For Black Power, A Moral, Political, and Economic Imperative for the Twenty-First Century*, (Brooklyn, NY: Afrikan World InfoSystem, 1998), 2.

their own schools to educate their children to think for themselves and unleash their creativity; they need their own hospitals to treat their sick, and their own supermarkets to ensure they have healthy food available to their community. To accomplish this, there needs to be a reengineering of black people's minds to release them from the shackles of oppression.

The purpose of this book is to point out what black people must do for themselves because America will not give them what they must give themselves: love, cooperation, socioeconomic power, and independence. Taught to hate themselves and not cooperate with themselves, the test of black people's resilience to move from survival to liberation is on display in the eyes of the world. With God's help, black people have an opportunity to show what they can do to recapture the greatness of their ancestors who built the pyramids and ruled dynasties and kingdoms, and, in the highlight of all progress. All of this was arrested, crucified and buried during the African diaspora. However, wherever there is a crucifixion, there must be a resurrection. It is time for the resurrection of black people, especially here in America, to rise from the dust of humiliation to the destiny of socioeconomic political power. Maya Angelou prophetically said:

> You may write me down in history.
> With your bitter, twisted lies,
> You may trod me in the very dirt.
> But still, like dust, I'll rise.[4]

This resurrection is not based upon hate, violence, and revenge against those who put black people in this unhealthy social, economic, and political condition for centuries, but based on love, justice, dignity, and humanity to show themselves and the Western world a better way of doing things and a better way of running the world. Socioeconomic independence is the best kind of revenge. Black people did not go through horrific suffering for nothing. If there is such a thing as redemptive suffering, black people must exemplify it as Jesus did centuries ago.

For over 400 years, black people have tried to prove themselves to America, and still, they are—by and large—victims of oppression, systemic

---

4. Maya Angelou, *Still I Rise*, https://www.poetryfoundation.org. 1994.

racism, exploitation, police brutality, and killings. The energy put into trying to prove to oppressors black worth and black humanity should now be put into focusing on liberating and healing themselves and controlling their own destiny. "More specifically to the point, no matter how we choose to explain white oppression or global supremacy, whether cosmologically or mundanely, the ultimate reason the White Man does what he does is because he possesses the power to do so. The reason why the Black Man is victimized by White power is because he has not developed the power to prevent his victimization."[5] It is time for black people to develop power because there is no doubt that America will never correct the wrongs done to black people in any significant way. Although talks are underway about reparations, America may never pay reparations no more than Pharaoh was willing to pay reparations to the Hebrew slaves. If it weren't for divine subterfuge, the Hebrew slaves would have left Egypt empty-handed. There is never the desire nor the will of the oppressor to stop his oppression. This can only be done by the oppressed's unwillingness to cooperate with oppression. As long as the oppressed cooperate with their oppression, the oppressor will continue to oblige. Frederick Douglass came to this conclusion when he stated, "Find out just what any people will quietly submit to, and you have found out the exact measure of injustice and wrong which will be imposed upon them, and these will continue till they are resisted with either words or blows, or with both. The limits of tyrants are prescribed by the endurance of those whom they oppress."[6]

Black people must understand America is too in love with money and power to give them a blueprint on how to be free and independent. This is something the oppressed must learn for themselves. Pharaoh cared nothing about the slaves other than what he could get out of them. Regardless of what the oppressed slaves could have done to prove themselves to Pharaoh, their loyalty, worth, and humanity, Pharaoh would never accept or treat them as equals. Pharaoh would never give them justice, equality and reparations for their many years of slavery. It didn't happen then, and it won't happen now. America is in the trillions of dollars of debt, and the debt ceiling is raised every year to pay its bills. The likelihood that reparations will be paid to

---

5. Ibid., 2.

6. John Blassingame, *The Frederick Douglass Papers, series Three, Speeches, Debates, and Interviews*, Vol. 3, 1855–63 (New Haven: Yale University Press, 1985), 204.

the descendants of slaves from a nation already in the trillions of dollars of debt is probably not going to happen. Is there evidence that America paid reparations to other groups? Yes! America paid reparations to slave masters, the Jews, the Japanese, and native Americans. Will America finally pay reparations to its most loyal black citizens? Probably not! Since black people don't know when reparations will be paid or when justice is a reality for them in America, black people cannot wait any longer to carve out an economic, social, and political structure for themselves within this American structure, as Jews, Asians, and other racial groups have done. They must do what is necessary to become a people of socioeconomic political power. When God liberated the Hebrew slaves from Pharaoh, God never focused His attention on healing and repairing Pharaoh. God's attention was on liberating, healing, and getting His people to their Promised Land. The laws God gave to His people were for their benefit, not for the benefit of Pharaoh and Egypt.

Therefore, black people must free themselves from their American Pharaoh by taking control of their own future and destiny. They must not trust Pharaoh because he will change his mind concerning them. They must not trust his smiles, trust his promises, trust his pats on the back, trust the positions and titles he gives them because he will change his mind about them. When Pharaoh changes his mind about a people, the laws meant to protect them have no power.

History reveals that Pharaoh changes his mind concerning the oppressed, but as long as God doesn't change His mind concerning the oppressed, there is still hope. It doesn't matter how powerful Pharaoh is, God is All power; it doesn't matter how mighty Pharaoh is, God is Almighty. God is our refuge and strength, a very present help in trouble . . . Though the earth be removed, and though the mountains be carried in the midst of the sea; . . . The Lord of hosts is with us; the God of Jacob is our refuge" (Psalms 46).

As long as black people look to their oppressor as the prototype of power, respect, and submission, they will never develop into the type of people God would have them to be. They must realize the talk of liberty and justice for all has not been applied to black people thus far in America, and they can no longer wait for liberty and justice to be applied to them. They must provide this for themselves. Without socioeconomic and political power, black America will always be at the mercy of other racial groups for jobs and services. They must act with a fierce sense of urgency to avoid becoming slaves to society and viewed as a race of beggars. It is time for black America to unite and develop a strategy to overcome the barriers it faces. America knows systemic racism is wrong, but it is unwilling to correct it. They know police treatment of black people is far different from that of white people. America knows what has been done to black people is unfair, unjust, and inhumane, yet they don't have the will to correct the problem. It is not a matter of not knowing the historical and contemporary wrongs and atrocities against black people. It is a matter of not caring to make right what is done wrong to black people. America knows, but practices self-imposed ignorance to overlook the social, economic, educational, and political injustice against black people. A few whites have tried to help turn the tide of oppression against black people, but not enough to transform the system designed to exploit and oppress them.

Consequently, the future of black people lies within their own hands. Frederick Douglass said, "No man can be truly free whose liberty is dependant upon the thought, feelings, and actions of others, and who has himself no means in his own hands for guarding, protecting, defending, and maintaining that liberty."[7] Black people must prove to themselves that they can stand on their own, run their own affairs, and control their own destiny. Black people have been working, waiting, praying, hoping, and wailing for over 400 years for justice, equality, and dignity to be a reality in their collective lives, but their efforts have fallen short because they are up against structural powers. Before desegregation, black people were forced to create a nation within a nation; they had their own banks, schools, hospitals, food markets, and other businesses that produced with prosperity everything the black community needed to help them in their social and economic rise. Today, they have become total consumers. Desegregation destroyed black people's faith in their own ability to stand on their own without the interference of the white oppressor giving them approval and direction. Black people must face the fact that they have been hoodwinked and bamboozled into powerlessness, and unless they recreate a socioeconomic power structure for themselves, they have no future.

---

7. Frederick Douglass, *The Life and Times of Frederick Douglass* (New York: Pathway Press, 1941), 345.

Once again, black people must become a Wall Street across this nation with all the safeguards in place to protect themselves and their property. They must never allow what happened in Tulsa, Oklahoma, in 1921, where whites totally burned down their community and businesses and killed black people, ever to happen again. There were other places where this terrorism was like what happened in Tulsa, Oklahoma. Terrorism has been part of black people's sojourn while trying to gain freedom and justice in America. It is shameful that over 406 years later, black people are still experiencing similar treatment as they have experienced in the past. Is there hope? Yes! But this hope lies within black people, who are their own solution to their collective socioeconomic and political problems. Socioeconomic Independence is one of the great solutions to a collective complicated problem!

People may ask, "Will this approach undercut the integration of black people in America?" No other racial group, such as the Jews, Asians, Indians, or Arabs, would be asked this question. Furthermore, black people have not achieved integration; they've achieved assimilation. They never had true integration. True integration is when coequal powers come together without either one losing anything culturally, spiritually, socially, economically, or educationally. Black people have never had coequal power with their oppressors; therefore, they have assimilated, not integrated into the dominant culture of their oppressors. In the process of assimilation or camouflaged integration, black people have lost most of their community, social, economic, religious, and educational cohesiveness that made them distinct as a racial group. Many scholars, like Claud Anderson, confirm the fact that integration did cause a great drain in the black community:

> Once blacks began to integrate, they abandoned their businesses, schools, and communities; they also lost disposable capital that is now redirected to white communities; they even lost their middle-class black role models, who followed whites to the suburbs. The loss of black capital and role models has left black communities across the nation impoverished and without leadership. And, worst of all, under integration, black people have had to shape their goals, values and behavior around white America's

standards, though whites' approval likely will not reap financial or political gains for black people.[8]

Amos Jones, Jr., also recognized what black people lost under this new social order of camouflaged integration.

> Integration that has come to mean annihilation, rising unemployment, removal of educational institutions from black communities and control, erosion of social progress and social programs gained in the sixties, mounting cases of injustice in the courts the land, and a sweeping mood of conservatism in the likes of the Moral Majority movement and the reappearance of the Ku Klux Klan—all have thrown black people into a state of shock, disbelief, and disorientation. The vision of the Promised Land that Martin Luther King, Jr., saw, toward which black feet invincibly marched, has suddenly vanished.[9]

To liberate themselves from the people who hold the wealth and the whip, black people must become a people of power. This strategic goal may conflict with the dominant class because those who oppress and exploit don't want the dominated to be independent and competitive with them. This is what brought on the American Revolution. America did not want to be oppressed, controlled, and exploited by the British Empire. America fought and won, and, with the help of Black people, became an independent nation. Black America must do the same for themselves to break the economic, social, and political stronghold the system has over them, and become economically independent first, then work towards interdependence. The goal is to become a people of power, and if this causes conflict in the process, it is no more than the conflict America had with the British Empire. Reinhold Niebuhr said, "Conflict is inevitable, and in this conflict, power must be challenged by power."[10] The conflict I am talking about is not with guns and bombs, but organizing collective mass

---

8. Claud Anderson, *Black Labor White Wealth, The Search for Power and Economic Justice,* (PowerNomics Corporation of America, 1994), 54.

9. Amos Jones, Jr., *Paul's Message of Freedom What Does It Mean to the Black* Church (Valley Forge, PA: Judson Press, 1984), 121–122.

10. Reinhold Niebuhr, *Moral Man and Immoral Society, A Study in Ethics and Politics,* (New York: Charles Scribner's Sons, 1932), xv.

social, economic, and political action to transform the black community. Unfair policies keep black people disadvantaged. Black America must fight for itself and not apologize for gaining power, because power is needed to change a people's reality. When we talk about power, "It is not simply the ability to get something done, but to get it done despite the resistance and opposition of others."[11]

It is not what a nation says but what it does that matters. The Constitution of the United States was written by white people, of white people, and for white people. The 13th through the 15th Amendments to the Constitution were written to put an end to slavery, to give blacks protection under the law, and to give them voting rights. These amendments are not being enforced because to this day, efforts, plans, and strategies are constantly employed to keep black people from benefiting from these amendments. With enlightenment, black people must stop participating in the plans and strategies against them. Without trying to become a people of power, black America sets itself up to be a slave to society. The time has come for black America to close ranks, preoccupy itself with its own liberation, healing, and gaining and maintaining collective power. Gaining power should be the goal of the 21st century. To achieve this, black people must free their minds from the shackles of slavery and put their minds under Jesus Christ, the true Liberator!

Martin Luther King, Jr. attempted to make economic power a major strategy of the Civil Rights Movement, but he did not live long enough to see it through. It was a missed opportunity of the Civil Rights movement, but black America and its leadership should make sure they don't miss this opportunity again. Black America today must understand that everything done to them by their oppressors was an effort to gain power, wealth, and control over people and resources. Black people were the workforce needed to achieve this goal. Now that black people have made their oppressors rich and powerful, it is time for them to make themselves rich and powerful. The goal is not assimilation nor integration but aggregation, a coming together in unity to pool all economic, social, educational, and spiritual resources to stop the power of racism and oppression against them. Black people have enriched Whites, Indians, Arabs, Asians, Koreans, Chinese,

---

11. Thomas Sowell, cited from Claud Anderson, *Black Labor White Wealth*, 29.

and others by supporting their businesses but these racial groups have not supported black businesses and causes for their socioeconomic uplift. Black people can no longer afford lifting others while they are still trapped at the bottom. Self-care and achieving power must be the focus of black people in this 21st century.

To do what is suggested requires courage, intentionality, and organization. Stokely Carmichael said, "Organization is necessary because oppressed people have never defeated their oppressors without it . . . organization allows us to correctly interpret the true nature of our oppression and how it affects the political, economic, and cultural reality our lives and to educate the people as to what we are fighting against and what we are fighting for."[12] Black America has worked hard for the progress of this nation; it is time to work hard for its own progress without apology. The clock of America's promises to black people has ticked out. Black America must think, strategize, and plan for itself going forward in the twenty-first century. They must not trust America to keep any promises to them. God never liberated His people for them to be controlled by their oppressors. This is the reason the Apostle Paul said, "Stand fast therefore in the liberty by which Christ has made us free, and do not be entangled again with a yoke of bondage" (Galatians 5:1).

The reason black people in America have not progress as much as they could have is they allowed themselves to get entangled again in the promises, lies, myths, and ideas of America that have never considered them equal nor given them a just educational, social and economic start to catch up with the rest of the nation. When it seems there is racial and social progress, there is always a white backlash that follows, and this has been throughout American history, such as Reconstruction, affirmative action, DEI etc. People may argue that a few blacks have occupied many powerful and prestigious positions in America. This is true, they have, but the few cannot compensate for the many. Unless all blacks are free and treated with justice, equality, and dignity, it is inauthentic for the few. A few blacks can't create the power needed for black people to be socioeconomically independent. It takes all black people to achieve this. Black people cannot allow themselves to be disunited again. They must stick together at all costs.

---

12. Stokely Carmichael, *Ready For Revolution*, (New York: Scribner Publisher, 2003), 678.

My appeal to black people is that God has seen our affliction in America as He had seen the affliction of His people in Egypt. God knows our sorrow, suffering, and pain. After 406 years, God is in the process of delivering us from the socioeconomic system of oppression. To gain full liberation in America, we must cooperate with God through Jesus Christ and with ourselves. We have successfully come through two emancipations, and we have one more to go. The one more to go will either retard our progress or propel it. The one more emancipation is the hardest of them all because it is psychological. The chains that were on the hands and feet are now on the mind. God, through Christ, wants to work through black people's minds to liberate them from the effects and trauma of racism, miseducation, and oppression by first healing them psychologically. When they are psychologically healed, everything else will fall into place for their full liberation.

Let me give a warning signal as black America moves forward in this 21st century, and in this current time of American backlash. The reason the children of Israel died in the wilderness is that they refused to allow God to heal them psychologically. They wanted to go back to their place of suffering and death. The children of Israel would not remove from their minds Pharaoh, the garlic, the tomatoes, and the flash pots of Egypt. Pharaoh had a grip on their minds, and God sought to free them by showing them His power over Pharaoh and Egypt. Due to their fear and refusal to undergo psychological emancipation, the initial people who marched out of Egypt died in the wilderness. After 40 years of being in the wilderness, only Joshua and Caleb from this initial group of Israelites made it to the Promised Land. This is the very reason I am lifting up this important emancipation for oppressed people, because they will never be free until their minds are liberated from their oppressor's ideas, suggestions, and presuppositions. Unless the oppressed undergo decolonization of the mind, they will continue to cooperate with their oppression. They will continue to desire Pharaoh more than their own liberation.

Because I believe it is time for the bottom rail to come to the top, as was prophesied by black ancestors, black people must "Humble themselves, and pray, and seek God's face, and turn from their wicked ways, then they will hear from heaven, and their sins forgiven, and experience the healing of the land" (2 Chronicles 7:14). In this book, I want to show that new forms of slavery can be avoided when black people apply the right therapy for their diagnosis. The late William R. Jones always taught how "The diagnosis dictates the therapy," and if we get both spot on, a new reality could happen in the life of a disinherited people. I want to make it clear that my diagnosis is not new. It is not another paradigm shift. Other black authors have pointed this out in some way, form or fashion. I want to turn up the volume as loud as it can go to get black people to understand that the problem of racism and oppression at its core is the problem of power. Power is what is needed to stop the power against the people. Unless black people in this 21st century put their energy into harnessing socioeconomic power, they don't stand a chance of being a competitive racial group. Moral suasion is a wonderful influence, but unless you have power, moral suasion won't be enough. Moses' words meant nothing to Pharaoh until he backed them up with power. Martin Luther King, Jr. came to understand this in 1967. He said, "The problem of transforming the ghetto, therefore, is a problem of power . . . Now power properly understood is nothing but the ability to achieve purpose. It is the strength required to bring about social, political, and economic change."[13] One thing is clear: black people cannot gain power by giving over their economics to those who oppress them and cannot expect their oppressors to give them a blueprint for liberation.

After 430 years, the children of Israel finally made their exodus out of Egypt. It has been 400-plus years for Black people in America. There is something about 400. There was a 400-year silence between the Old and New Testaments. I believe the Almighty God is working to lead black people out of their long night of oppression. Geographically, it may not be to leave the land of their oppressors, like in the case with the Israelites, but to establish them in the land of their oppression with power and authority to control their own destiny. I believe the prophecy that says, "Ethiopia shall stretch out of her hand to God; . . . from beyond the rivers of Ethiopia will I receive my dispersed ones; they shall bring me sacrifice," (Psalms 68:31). Black America stands on the precipice of a new reality, and this book can be a guidepost and a warning. Both are needed to get to the destination of full liberation.

---

13. Martin Luther King, Jr., *A Testament of Hope The Essential Writings of Martin Luther King, Jr.,* edited by James Melvin Washington (San Francisco: Harper & Row, 1986), 246.

Chapter One

THE FIRST AND GREATEST EMANCIPATION CAME THROUGH JESUS CHRIST

It is for freedom that Christ has set us free. Stand firm, then, and do not let yourselves be burdened again by a yoke of slavery.

—GALATIANS 5:1

Who better to understand structural oppression than the person born into oppression? Jesus Christ was born in oppression, nurtured in discrimination, and socialized in the inferiority proscriptions imposed upon him and his community. He was a product of his time when Rome occupied Palestine. Though he was born and raised in oppression, he went around doing good by healing the sick, raising the dead, and giving sight to the blind. Jesus brought and taught the Kingdom of God and its principles to unite an oppressed and powerless people to liberate them. He could not free them without their participation. Liberation is made even more difficult when the oppressed have made peace with their oppression.

Because oppressed people are mostly religious people, Jesus rejected institutional religion, which was a prop for oppression. Many people listened to him. He made it crystal clear what his mission and objectives were. "The Spirit of the Lord is on me, because he has anointed me to proclaim good news to the poor. He has sent me to proclaim freedom for the prisoners and recover of sight for the blind, to set the oppressed free, to proclaim the year of the Lord's favor" (Luke 4:18). Jesus's whole objective was liberation. Anything that held people captive culturally, socially, economically, religiously, and spiritually, Jesus's aim was to liberate people from it.

But liberation must be taught; it must be demonstrated so the oppressed can participate in it. When the oppressed don't fully understand the mapping and trapping of oppression, they could easily cooperate with it, not knowing they are doing so. Therefore, liberation must be taught and applied to counter the everyday entrapments of oppression. When Jesus taught and applied the principles of the Kingdom of God in the context of oppression, the liberation movement started to grow. The owners and gatekeepers of institutional oppression began to see Jesus as a threat, a dangerous revolutionary who must be stopped and his influence extinguished. Jesus was more concerned about the liberation of the oppressed than he was about his own death. He knew that his life was in constant danger because anytime you are liberating people from the entrapments of oppression, when oppressors are greatly benefiting from that oppression, oppressors will kill to protect their interests. Jesus was very much aware that his movement was creating conflict and disturbing the status quo. He told those around him and those in power who needed to hear him, "Do not suppose that I have come to bring peace to the earth. I did not come to bring peace, but a sword" (Matthew 10:34).

Jesus made it known that he did not come to play the game of oppression; he did not come to compromise with oppressors, nor plead and beg for justice and liberation for the oppressed. He brought a sword, meaning gathering and organizing the oppressed to overcome their oppression and achieve total liberation. Anybody who wants to join this movement in this effort is welcome to do so; anybody who wants to play politics, compromise with oppressors, and make under-the-table deals is not welcome. Jesus made it clear, "No one can serve two masters. Either you will hate the one and love the other, or you will be devoted to the one and despise the other. You cannot serve both God and money" (Matthew 6:24). Not that money is evil in itself, but the lover of money makes people sell out the cause of liberation. Money is only a tool, and it can be used for right or wrong reasons. The oppressed must organize their money for their liberation and restoration, and not allow themselves to be sold out by money.

Therefore, since money and its power could not influence Jesus to compromise with oppressors, the next step was to get rid of him. Anytime money cannot be used to get liberators to sell out the people, that same money is used to get rid of liberators. Unless Jesus is annihilated, his liberation movement would set the oppressed free, and oppressors wouldn't have anyone to oppress and exploit to further their interests. Efforts were set in motion to kill Jesus because when you destroy the mover of the movement, you can put a monument in his place to pacify the oppressed. What oppressors and their gatekeepers did not know was that Jesus was not only a Palestinian Jew, but he was the Son of God who had resurrection power to reverse the power of death. Thinking that the death of Jesus would be the death of the liberation movement, it gave life to it. The death of Jesus achieved the very thing oppressors were threatened by: the liberation of the oppressed. When Jesus was crucified on the Roman cross and said, "It is finished," the sin debt was paid, and mankind is now justified before God through the resurrection of Jesus Christ. The broken connection between God and His people is now restored, and together, through Christ, they can crush injustice and oppression. Since Jesus Christ is now sitting on the right hand of Power, the oppressed have the full power of the resurrection to gain the rest of their earthly liberation. The goal and objective of Jesus have not changed. Liberation is the goal. The only difference is that Jesus is sitting in a high, elevated place to assist the oppressed to break free from all forms of oppression.

Because of what Jesus Christ has done for humanity, God's people are to "Stand fast in the liberty by which Christ has made us free, and do not be entangled again with a yoke of bondage" (Galatians 5:1). Jesus Christ has made us free, and we should not get entangled again by systems, establishments, and institutions that oppress. God's people should not allow themselves to get into any form of bondage again. They should not participate in any doctrine, philosophy, or nationalism that enslaves them ever again. Jesus Christ has made us free, and we ought not to bow down to any man or any system that does not recognize this freedom we have in Jesus Christ. God's beloved Son of Africa has emancipated us. This is our first and greatest emancipation. We are responsible for protecting and enhancing our freedom through Christ by any means necessary. Although Christ freed us, black people were captured and sold into another bondage called American slavery. It was beyond their control to stop the middle passage from happening. They didn't have organized power or weaponry to stop the dehumanization and transportation of human cargo. They were captured and brought to America to be slaves in perpetuity. This bondage denied their humanity; it denied their education; it denied them justice and equality. Black people had no control over their bodies, families, or their destiny. They were totally under the control of their slave masters. The freedom Christ achieved for them was also denied, and reading, writing, and education for them were against the law. They were held in this wretched condition for over two and a half centuries.

While in bondage, black people were socialized and conditioned to think a certain way, act a certain way, and deal with each other a certain way. Black consciousness was hijacked, shaped, and bent to carry out a program not in their best interest. They were taught to hate themselves and not cooperate with themselves as a strategy to maintain oppression. American history was taught in such a way as to help black people see reality from the perspective of the oppressor. Amos Wilson stated, "We must be maintained in a particular state of mind. In a sense, then, we literally must be out of our minds—and we must be kept out of our minds."[14] To keep black people out of their minds, oppressors deposited in them certain beliefs and values that worked to the advantage of the oppressor but to the detriment of the oppressed. Whenever oppressors have total control over the minds of the oppressed, for example, through images, media, visible, and subliminal messages, the oppressed can be held in bondage indefinitely. Many black people have internalized their oppression to the point that they despise themselves, and to this day, they won't cooperate with themselves and are destroying themselves. This is the reason black people cannot build wealth and create power for themselves. They have not purged themselves of the consciousness deposited in them by their oppressors.

---

14. Amos N. Wilson, *The Falsification of AfriKan Consciousness*, (Brooklyn, NY: African World InfoSystems, 1993), 66.

Until this purging of the consciousness happens, "The fear of trusting and uniting with each other, the fear of coming together and solving our problems together and overcoming the dominance of European imperialism itself becomes a part of the problem and helps to maintain the system. Others try to deal with the discrepancy between what the system says they can achieve and our failure to achieve by lowering their personal aspirations, by, in a sense, fitting into a lesser place that the society reserves for them. Others try to inflate their achievements, to inflate their personalities."[15] The falsification of black people's indoctrination must be confronted head-on if transformation and liberation are to be realities in the lives of black people in America, and ultimately around the world. A psychological metamorphosis would give black people "Inner freedom, and then, inevitably, outer freedom, for once the people acquired individual dignity, they would insist on better living, and nobody would hold them in bondage."[16] Chancellor Williams believed succeeding generations of black youth could be the answer to the collective problems of black people if they were properly awakened. To undo what has taken centuries to build in the minds of black people may have caused doubt, but black youth are generating hope that mental decolonization is possible, though it will take time to accomplish.

> That Caucasianization of the Blacks was so well done over so many centuries that it is doubtful if real liberation of our minds will be achieved in this generation. Yet the black youth in the 1960s brought about the greatest reversal of the race's attitude toward itself ever achieved. There is, therefore, no grounds for despair and much ground for faith if we understand that total liberation will be slow even with the best efforts and that there will always be those who have the white viewpoint on race and will never abandon it. These cannot stop the onward march of the whole people to human equality and dignity. But who will begin to lay the first stone in the foundation of the greatest movement for racial unity and power ever undertaken?[17]

---

15. Ibid., 75.

16. Louis Fisher, *Mahatma Gandhi, Gandhi His Life and Message for the World* (New York: The New American Library, A Signet Key Book, 1954), 54.

17. Chancellor Williams, *The Destruction of Black Civilization Great Issues Of A Race From 4500 B.C. To 2000 A.D.*, (Hawthorne, CA: BN Publishing, 2012), 347.

To answer Chancellor Williams's question about who will begin to lay the first stone in the foundation of racial unity and power is none other than Jesus Christ. Jesus Christ set us free and laid the first stone in the foundation of liberation. Black people in this 21st century have an opportunity to join Jesus Christ in the transformation of the effects of their slavery and oppression. Every generation must decide to join Jesus Christ in this liberation struggle. God, through Christ, worked through the abolitionist movement. God stood up a slave by the name of Frederick Douglass and put coals of fire in his soul, and he became an eloquent voice against slavery. Douglass spent his whole life breaking the chains of ignorance wherever they supported slavery and oppression. In his effort to see black people rise from the low pitiful state of slavery, Douglass said, "I have urged upon them self-reliance, self-respect, industry, perseverance, and economy—to make the best of both worlds, but to make the best of this world first because it comes first—and that he who does not improve himself by the motives and opportunities afforded by this world gives the best evidence that he would not improve in any other world."[18] Douglass encouraged blacks never to allow themselves to be enslaved again, and one way to avoid this is not to depend on others for their livelihood. Self-reliance is key to becoming a person of power. Once people have power, they can stop the power against them that wants to continue to oppress, exploit, and destroy them.

God called up Harriet Tubman and gave her navigational expertise, which she used to free slaves through the Underground Railroad. She later stated, "Now I've been free, I know what a dreadful condition slavery is. I have seen hundreds of escaped slaves, but I never saw one who was willing to go back and be a slave."[19] To expand this unwillingness to go back and be a slave, black America must understand this is exactly what is happening to them when they give all of their hard-earned resources to others outside of themselves. When black people don't carve out their own path to securing their freedom by gaining power for themselves, they are allowing themselves to be slaves to institutions, industries and corporations of

---

18. Frederick Douglass, *Life And Times of Frederick Douglass* (New York: Macmillan Publishing Company, 1962), 480.

19. Harriet Tubman, *The Refugee: Or the Narratives of Fugitive Slaves in Canada*, edited by Benjamin Drew (Boston: John P. Jewett and Company, 1856), 30.

society. Frederick Douglass, Harriet Tubman, and countless others, to our contemporary times, are working so that black people can have the full experience of total liberation. This can only happen when black people invest in themselves and control their destiny. But black people must understand that the enemy of the race is always plotting and planning to undermine whatever progress the race is making. If black people are not careful, coming out of one form of slavery can start a new form of slavery. If safeguards are not in place to prevent it, black people can be socially engineered into a new reality.

Despite the fact that ending physical slavery was a long and bitter struggle, physical freedom for the slaves eventually came. The forces of justice were moving, the voices of human rights were being heard, and the tension between the North and South came to a boil, forcing Abraham Lincoln on January 1, 1863, to issue a second emancipation for black people called "The Emancipation Proclamation." Although this emancipation was anemic in nature, black people were freed but still not free. They were still slaves to society, and forces were in place to ensure they never reached equality. The policy of Reconstruction that was enacted to help newly freed slaves get a fresh start ended as quick as it started. It lasted less than fifteen years. It was a cruel jest to give a few years of Reconstruction to a people held in slavery for 250 years. Reconstruction was struck down by a new policy called the "Great Compromise." Corruption and white supremacy kissed each other, and black people were pushed into a new form of slavery. Sharecropping became the new system of oppression. The old slaveowners were now the new landowners issued by the federal government. Jim Crow was enacted, separate and unequal, and black people had to struggle another one hundred years to achieve civil and voting rights in the 1960s. Black people have experienced two emancipations. One which Jesus Christ has achieved for humanity, and the second is the Emancipation Proclamation of 1863, and all of the constitutional amendments that came with it, to include black people.

Now, black people have one more emancipation to go, and this one may be the hardest and most challenging. This one cannot be accomplished by anyone but blacks themselves. No sympathizers or group, or foreign power can do this for black people. They must accomplish this one for themselves. To heal themselves from the many years of the trauma of slavery that gives rise to the capture of their minds that causes them to hate themselves, not cooperate with themselves, sell out themselves, not think for themselves, not trust themselves, and not do for themselves, is worse than the shackles on the wrists and on the ankles. To remove the deep-rooted disturbance, the post-traumatic stress syndrome caused by slavery and transgenerational oppression, black people must undergo psychological emancipation. They must write this prescription for themselves because they are a 2 trillion-dollar people who are still dealing with mental issues that prevent them from rising to become a people of socioeconomic power. There is a controversy about the 2 trillion dollar buying power of black people of which I will discuss later in this book. But whatever the exact amount is in the collective hands of black people, they must put this to their own liberation and socioeconomic uplift. If they are going to pull themselves out of the quicksand of hopelessness to the solid rock of possibility, if they are going to have victory over racism and oppression, and conquer powerlessness, hopelessness, joblessness, and a false consciousness that produces madness in their communities, they must undergo psychological emancipation. The white consciousness inculcated in them must be replaced by a newly informed consciousness that releases their greatness and creative power.

Their self-transformation hinges on their mental emancipation. Although getting a very late start due to slavery and oppression, the 21st century is probably the last opportunity they may have to liberate their minds from the psychological effects of slavery. Unless the shackles on their minds are removed, they cannot achieve healing, self-sufficiency, and total liberation. Unless the mind is emancipated, people will voluntarily go back and serve their abusers, oppressors, and those who harm them. When the oppressed know more about the history, aims, goals, and well-being of the oppressors and desire to know nothing about their true history or what they can become, the rehabilitation of the mind is the first step in the process of liberation. "Oppression requires the dissociation of the oppressed from themselves; that they deny themselves, in service to their oppressors; that they avoid identifying with their original personality and perceive identification with it as detrimental to their survival. The rejection of their authentic selves on the part of the oppressed is a necessary preparatory step to their replacement by artificial, manipulable selves socially manufactured by their oppressors."[20]

Moses discovered this: Unless oppressed people undergo psychological emancipation, they will find it difficult to let Pharaoh go. Moses spent 40 years in the wilderness trying to get his people to let Pharaoh go. Why did they desire to go back and serve Pharaoh? Why did they have more faith in what Pharaoh could do for them than what they could do for themselves? Why did they desire to go back to the same hellhole they cried for God to deliver them from? The answer: they never underwent psychological emancipation. They preferred the fleshpots of Egypt to the milk and honey of the Promised Land. They did what Paul warned not to do, "Become entangled again with the yoke of bondage." To achieve wholeness of the mind, body, and spirit of a people, psychological emancipation should be their struggle and aim. When the minds of the oppressed are freed, their self-definition, unity, and money, creativity, and self-determination are freed from the domination of their oppressors. But, until this type of psychological emancipation is achieved, all the gains made will be lost, and the freed people can be entangled again with the yoke of bondage.

Carter G. Woodson was spot on when he said, "The problem of holding the Negro down is easily solved. If you control a man's thinking, you do not have to worry about his actions. You do not have to tell him not to stand here and go yonder. He will find his "proper place" and stay in it. You do not have to send him to the back door. He will go without being told. In fact, if there is no back door, he will cut one for his special benefit. His education (his socialization, his religious indoctrination, and political orientation) makes it necessary."[21] Mental slavery is the worst kind of captivity. Fear is built into the minds of those held captive by oppressors. Black people must be intentional about liberating themselves from what their oppressors have inculcated in them. The 21st century and beyond depend on what black people are willing to do for themselves to become a people with socioeconomic and political power. Black people are doing well with spiritual-emotional power that fosters a vertical relationship with God to hang on for another day while being in a social and economic crisis, but now black

---

20. Amos Wilson, *The Falsification of Afrikan Consciousness*, 133.

21. Carter G. Woodson, *The Miseducation of the Negro* (Trenton, NJ: Africa World Press, Inc, 1933), xiii.

people must take this spiritual-emotional power and foster horizontally a relationship with themselves to become a people of socioeconomic political power to create and protect their interests now and in the future.

There is a story about a majestic bird that used to fly with all the freedom God had given it, until the day it was captured and put in a cage. Initially, the bird vigorously fought to free itself from the cage. Week after week, month after month, year after year, the bird struggled to free itself. But over time, the bird's mind began to accept his captivity. It accepted the fact that flying free again would never be a reality. Therefore, the bird stopped struggling because in its mind, the struggle would be useless. The bird's actions came into compliance with its mind, and it gave in to its predicament. Then, one day, the bird's captor decided to open the cage and let the bird go free. He removed the bird from the cage and noticed it refused to fly. He checked the bird's wings, its legs, and other parts of its body to see if there was any physical disability preventing the bird from flying. A veterinarian was called in to give the bird a thorough physical examination, but there was no sign of physical disability. Then they brought in a psychologist, who discovered that the bird's mind had been damaged. Until the bird's mind is treated and healed, it will never fly again because it believes it is still in the cage. If this kind of mental damage can happen to a bird, it can also happen to people.

Let me make it clear that black people are not in any way, form, or fashion inferior to any people. They have been a captured people who have gone through hell and back again while living in a racist and oppressive system that has treated them unjustly and unequal to this day. It is a truism that this racist treatment has affected the minds of black people to the point that many of them see themselves through the lens of their oppressors without getting their own lens to see themselves. Paulo Freire stated, "The oppressed, having internalized the image of the oppressor and adopted his guidelines, are fearful of freedom. Freedom would require them to eject this image and replace it with autonomy and responsibility. Freedom is acquired by conquest, not by gift . . . they prefer the security of conformity with their state of unfreedom to the creative communion produced by freedom and even the very pursuit of freedom."[22] All of this

---

22. Paulo Freire, *Pedagogy of the Oppressed* (New York: Continuum Press, 1999), 29–30.

stems from a consciousness shaped by the oppressor. Consciousness shaped by the oppressor contains a fear of self-reliance. Nothing should be done or pursued without the stamp of approval of the oppressor, and oppressors will never approve of the liberation and empowerment of the oppressed. "The ability of dominant Whites to socially manufacture or markedly influence Afrikan states of consciousness and conduct in the interest of perpetuating white supremacy is both the source and product of the power relations and inequalities which inhere between these races. The White social manufacture of Black consciousness and behavior will end when the power differentials which make this process possible are equalized or reversed by the increased Black empowerment."[23]

Therefore, not only do black people have to change the way they think about themselves, but they must also get rid of the fear within themselves that stifles their determination for liberation. As the scripture says, "Whatsoever a man thinks, so is he" (Proverbs 23:7). Thus, if black people think they are grasshoppers, they are. If they think they are inferior to others, they are. If they think they cannot rise and recapture their greatness as a people, they won't. If they don't think and believe they can love themselves, trust themselves, and do business with themselves, they won't. If they think they cannot own and control their destiny, they cannot. If they think they cannot build an economic infrastructure in their community to provide jobs and services for their own people, they cannot. If they think they cannot move from chaos to community, from dependency to self-sufficiency, they will never break free from those things that cause their nightmare and pending holocaust. The work of liberation is harder than slavery. The late Miles Monroe said, "When oppression becomes a mental condition, then physical freedom is not enough . . . The mind is the key to life . . . Therefore, your mental state is more important than your physical state. You are not free until your mind is liberated. Freedom is first a mental condition before it is a physical statement . . . Of course, it's tough to change—without mental transformation, the actions we take to 'change' may only produce a new place where we continue to do our old things."[24]

---

23. Amos Wilson, *The Falsification of Afrikan Consciousness, Eurocentric History, Psychiatry and the Politics of White Supremacy* (New York: Afrikan World InfoSystems Publisher, 1993), 113.

24. Myles Monroe, *The Burden of Freedom Discover the Keys to Your Individual and National Freedom* (Lake Mary, FL: Charisma House A Strang House, 2000, 2001), 7, 19.

Enslaved people can be physically freed, but the minds of the oppressed can only be freed by the oppressed themselves. Oppressed people must be willing to dump and discard what they have learned from their oppressors, or otherwise they will carry out the oppressor's program while maintaining their own oppression. Until black people undergo psychological emancipation, the nihilism we see among black people will only get worse. Martin Luther King, Jr. stated, "As long as the mind is enslaved, the body can never be free. Psychological freedom, a firm sense of self-esteem, is the most powerful weapon against the long night of physical slavery. No Lincolnian emancipation proclamation, Kennedyan, or Johnsonian civil rights bill can fully bring this kind of freedom. The Negro will only be truly free when he reaches down to the inner depths of his own being and signs with pen and ink of assertive selfhood his own emancipation proclamation."[25]

Psychological emancipation may be the hardest and the most challenging, but it is key to the future of black America and the future of their children and children's children. Black people must break the chains of psychological slavery, and when they achieve this emancipation, they put themselves on a trajectory of becoming a people of socioeconomic and political power. Once they erase from their consciousness the concepts, beliefs, and values of their oppressors that produce distrust and disdain for themselves, they can build and control their own destiny by building new pyramids and new wonders of the world, as their ancestors did millennia ago. Developing a new consciousness leads to a new reality for black people. They must continue to cast off images and definitions that have hindered their unity and psychological healing. The critical variable is mind transformation, which would prevent them from getting entangled again in the yoke of bondage. The socialization and miseducation of black people have caused them to live out of their minds. For blacks to constantly destroy themselves, refuse to cooperative with themselves, not get involved in the education of their children, and give over their economic power to other ethnic groups while impoverishing themselves must be living out of their minds. Until the veil of ignorance is lifted from their eyes, they could easily enter a new form of slavery. NAIM AKBAR stated, "We are confident that

---

25. Martin Luther King, Jr., *Where Do We Go From Here: Chaos or Community?* (New York: Harper and Row, 1967), 43.

the last remaining obstacle to the complete mental liberation of African American people is the failure to release ourselves from slavery. What is now necessary for completion of our liberation cannot be accomplished by anyone but ourselves."[26]

To help in the process of freeing the mind requires moving away from the frames of reference set up by oppressors. These references keep the oppressed in the dark about themselves and their history. He who controls the references controls the narrative. A Zimbabwean proverb says, "Until the lion tells his side of the story, the tale of the hunt will always glorify the hunter."[27] Black people must take over their own narrative and not leave it to the oppressor group to do this for them. In grade and high schools, colleges, universities, seminaries, etc., black America must tell their own story to the world. Lerone Bennett Jr. stated:

> The overriding need for the moment is for [the oppressed] to think with [their] own mind. We cannot see now because our eyes are clouded by the concepts of white supremacy. We cannot think now because we have no intellectual instruments save those which were designed expressly to keep us from seeing. It is necessary for us to develop a new frame of reference, which transcends the limits of white concepts. White concepts have succeeded in making [oppressed] people feel inferior. White concepts have created the conditions that make it easy to dominate a people. The initial step towards liberation is to abandon the partial frame of reference of our oppressor and to create new concepts which release our reality.[28]

---

26. NAIM AKBAR, *Breaking The Chains of Psychological Slavery* (Tallahassee, FL: Mind Productions & Associates, 1996), ii.

27. Cited from Goodreads.com.

28. Lerone Bennett Jr. *The Challenge of Blackness*, (Chicago, IL: Johnson Publishing Company, 1972), 36.

Chapter Two

REBUILD THE BLACK FAMILY

For centuries, Black families have shouldered the ramifications of discrimination and structural racism. —April Thames

There is no gainsaying that slavery and today's transgenerational oppression have devastated the black family. The system of slavery tore parents from each other, tore children from their parents, and tore children from one another. This cruel act lasted throughout slavery, and it has scarred the psyche of black people and crippled their upward mobility. The pain and anguish of black people cannot really be described. It is beyond comprehension how a people could survive such inhumanity and still be here. There can only be something divine about a people to undergo such harsh treatment. No other racial group on this American soil has undergone this type of assault as the black family has.

Black husbands' wives and children were totally under the control of their white oppressors. They were never given the freedom to live out the biblical definition of the family. The black family has never really been stable because living in a racist, oppressive society, any slight infraction against the power structure could mean arrest, imprisonment, or death for the black family. The black family is in a constant state of instability and vulnerability. Being in this constant state, studies show that this affects the health of a people such as high blood pressure, heart disease, etc.

Although in this constant state, black people still must rebuild their families because they are the foundation of social unity to become a community of socioeconomic power. "The family is the very foundation of healthy, constructive, personal and community life. Without a strong family, individual life and community life are likely to become very unstable. The destruction or damage to the African American was accomplished by destroying marriage, fatherhood and motherhood."[29] Without major renovation on the foundation of the black community, which includes but is not limited to marriage, fatherhood, motherhood, home training, education, economic cooperation, and spiritual awareness, etc., the black community may self-destruct. The violence, the killings, the gangs, the drugs, are ingredients of self-destruction. Unless we conquer these present conditions, they will conquer us, and it would be ashame that our ancestors conquered ignorance and build civilizations, and ruled empires like Ghana, Mali, Songhai, and Zulu, but we could not conquer the conditions in our contemporary time.

Satan, the real enemy, is attacking the black community at its most vulnerable level, which is the black family. At the end of the day, the family is all a community has; destroy it, and there is no community. Therefore, at all costs, efforts ought to be made to strengthen the core of the community—the family. Robert Michael Franklin stated, "If we fail to get the family agenda right, we will take a tragic step backward in our heroic movement for justice and opportunity. In other words, much of the progress made during the post-Civil Rights movement years could be jeopardized by our inattention to the health of this primary anchor institution."[30] When the black family is strengthened, the community is strengthened, and it will have a domino effect on the whole of society. Amos Wilson made a very cogently observation about the need for the black family:

> The family is one such fundamental cultural subsystem. It is a system of social relations, hierarchical in structure, where different members exercise different privileges, prerogatives, and different levels of authority. The family is a primary organization, a fundamental generator or source of

---

29. NAIM AKBAR, *Breaking The Chains of Psychological Slavery*, 19.

30. Robert M.Franklin, *Crisis In The Village Restoring Hope in African American Communities* (Minneapolis, MN: Fortress Press, 2007), 42.

power where the human and non-human capital resources of its members are pooled and shared as means of achieving is vital goals . . . The family is a system where power is customarily and legally exercised; where its members are not only related by kinship ties, by blood and a shared history, but relate to each other in terms of membership rights, duties, behavioral expectations and authority. The character and personality of individual family members, especially its young, are developed, shaped, and continuously influenced by the organization and exercise of power and authority inside and outside the family unit.[31]

Like other family groups, such as the Jews, the Asians, and the Hispanics, who have created and maintained their family units for socioeconomic power, black people must do the same to have a respected foothold in this American empire. This is not to suggest that black people have not tried to build and maintain the black family before. They have and must rebuild again. The problem has been, and still is the forces of oppression have been a thorn in their side. But, despite the thorn of racism and oppression black people have been given, they must take the lemons and make lemonade and bricks out of straw. The hardships and difficulties facing the black community cannot be tackled without the rehabilitation of black families coming together to form a united front to create wealth and power to aid them in the quest for full liberation.

The concentration must be on rebuilding and repairing the black community by pooling resources, intelligence, trust, responsibility, accountability, and obedience to God through Jesus Christ. This must be done with intentionality. The process won't be easy because the culture dynamics in and around the black community have been less than desirable for a healthy family and community. Nevertheless, with God's help and black people's determination, a new standard of morality, decency, dignity, and economic and social power can be the new fabric of the black community as we advance in the 21st century.

Black people don't have to look at any other ethnic group to gain wisdom and understanding about how to rebuild the black family. There are

---

31. Amos Wilson, *Blue Print For Black Power, A Moral, Political, and Economic Imperative for the Twenty-First Century,* 57.

historical examples of strong black families before desegregation. What did the black family look like, and why do black people need to reimplement the model in today's time? The answer is to rebuild and thrive. Black people have done it before. Regardless of external restrictions of segregation, racism, and oppression, the black family unit, which is comprised of black men, women, children, and extended family, made up the black community. The overwhelmingly majority of black families had two-parent homes, in which each parent played out different roles. Usually, the wife stayed at home, managing the household and watching over the children, while the husband worked to make sure the family could at least eat and keep a roof over their heads. Only by necessity would the wife go outside the home to work to help maintain the family unit. Communal cooperation between the husband, wife, and extended family helped to ensure the family's survival in a restrictive, racist society. "Whereas Euro-American families are more compatible with individualism and materialism, African American families show an interdependence or communal cooperation born out of the necessity of providing a living."[32] This communal cooperation not only made the black family strong, but it also provided the psychological and emotional support needed to navigate through a racist society.

Another major component that made the black family strong was the role religion played in black families. Black families found strength and purpose in their lives when they came to their denominational churches. When they would sing and pray together, a sense of somebodiness and importance would enter their hearts and minds, and they believed God was with them despite external forces against them. Howard Thurman suggested that the church provided a somebodiness for black people who had been molested and buffeted about by their environment.[33] It was, and still is, a place to release their hurts, pains, and frustrations while keeping them connected to God and one another. "One must be sensitive to the role religion and spirituality have played in the lives of many African American people. The religious orientation is referred to as an awareness of and commitment to a spiritual lifestyle that provides a sense of power greater than

---

32. Littlejohn-Blake, Sheila M., and Carol Anderson Darling. "Understanding the Strengths of African American Families." Journal of Black Studies, vol. 23, no. 4, Sage Publications, Inc., 1993, pp. 460–71, http://www.jstor.org/stable/2784380.

33. Howard Thurman, *The Luminous Darkness* (Richmond, IN, Friends United Press, 1989), 21.

self. The belief held by most African American families that conditions will improve has been described as unfaltering faith and strong religious orientation . . . This system of core beliefs is the foundation of the inner strength of the people."[34] Black America needs to get back to its source of strength while forcing itself to become a people of socioeconomic power. Developing and repairing the village community of black families is key to becoming a powerful people.

As they did before, black people must work on laying the foundation for guiding principles at home. Too many young people have not had a foundation of guiding principles, and this is why their lives end up a train wreck. Unless discipline, respect, and responsibility are taught in the home, schools and churches alone cannot fill this void. The home is the greatest place to start children on the right path, and if children do not have a home or the home is dysfunctional, other resources in the black community must come to the rescue. Moral excellence must be constantly taught and demonstrated because too many young black girls are having children out of wedlock, and too many families are without black fathers. This dynamic is really hurting the black community. Many young black men in prison don't know their fathers, which adds another level of social pathology in the community. There is no way a community can rise without its black men. Jesus said, "No one can enter a strong man's house without first tying him up. Then he can plunder the strong man's house" (Mark 3:27). How can black families have any defense when many black men are not there to provide it? The black family has been plundered with father absenteeism, poverty, illiteracy, drugs, gangs, violence, and death. Without fathers in the home to control aggression, coupled with economic deprivation, discrimination, alienation, and emotional frustration, deviant behaviors are created among some black youth. Their aggressiveness against their own community is their explosive behaviors gone wild. Unless something is done to transform father absenteeism and create employment opportunities for black men, black families will continue to be plundered by socioeconomic ills. The black community is responsible for transforming its communities. The federal, state, and local governments can assist, but ultimately it is the responsibility of the

---

34. Littlejohn-Blake, Sheila M., and Carol Anderson Darling. "Understanding the Strengths of African American Families." *Journal of Black Studies*, vol. 23, no. 4, p. 461–462.

black community. W.E.B. Dubois stated, "It should continually impress the fact upon [black people] that they must not expect to have things done for them--they must do for themselves; that they have on their hands a vast work of self-reformation to do, and that a little less complaint and whining, and a little more dogged work and manly striving would do us more credit and benefit than a thousand Force or Civil Rights bill."[35]

It cannot be overstated that black men are desperately needed in the homes and in the black community. There is no question that slavery, racism, and structural inequality have played a role in the disenfranchisement of the black community, but most black men after slavery, during reconstruction, and during the civil rights movement stayed with their families, provided, and protected their families, and encouraged the children to get an education. Something went terribly wrong after the struggle for civil rights. It is my summation that after desegregation, there was an exodus of black culture, professionals, and economic resources that went out of the black communities to integrate into white communities. All of the major organs of the black community were removed, and the black community has been in the critical care unit ever since. This is one of the unintended consequences of the civil rights movement. It created a void that was filled with subculture values of fast money and bling-bling. The black community did the best it could to survive, but the values created by the void gave place to joblessness, nihilism, drugs, violence, depression, frustration, and father absenteeism. To this day, the black community is struggling against these economic and social psychological dynamics. The black community lost a lot of its valuable cultural and economic resources that helped to stabilize and give vision for black people. The unintended consequences of desegregation must be realized and corrected as we strategize going forward. Black people must get back to strengthening those areas that are leaving the black community vulnerable to the enemy they see and the enemy they cannot see. Closing the gaps in economic cooperation, unemployment, and father absenteeism can tremendously help a vulnerable community against destruction. By nature, men are providers and protectors, and the black community in a patriarchal society desperately needs strong men on every front of the community.

---

35. W.E.B. Dubois Speaks, Speeches And Address 1890-1919, edited by Philip S. Foner (Pathfinder Publisher, 1970), 82–83.

There is no way I would know what morality looks like, what manhood is, and what it means to provide and protect the family if it were not for seeing strong black men in the community. My father and supportive mother in the home provided moral and spiritual support to the children. Mother provided comfort, and father provided resources and regulated behavior. They demanded respect from the children, encouraged a relationship with God, and demonstrated the work ethic. Although father had a third-grade education, he had a Ph.D. in wisdom. I am who I am today because of his example in the home and in the community. Black people should never allow anybody to convince them that fathers don't matter in the homes and in the lives of their children and community. Jawanza Kunjufu stated, "We need fathers who will stay with their children. What do Tiger Woods, Shaq, Michael Jordan, and Venus and Serena Williams have in common? Beyond their talents and supportive mothers, they all had fathers who were driving forces in their lives. I challenge all fathers to learn from these great men."[36] This is not to devalue the great contribution of single-parent homes. There have been and still are great personalities who emerged from such homes. However, the goal is to get families back together and produce unity again in the future. God never intended for women and men to work separately. God wants the family together. God wants marriages to work to help advance His Kingdom on earth.

Notwithstanding, Satan and the demons of hell are at work to keep the black family and community crippled and powerless. Black people should not cooperate with the enemy but resist him at all times. Mahatma Gandhi said, "Non-cooperation with evil is as much a duty as cooperation with good."[37] Those things that are proving to keep the black community captive, such as sexual immorality, out-of-wedlock pregnancies, fatherlessness, divorce, gangs, drugs, violence, and death, ought to be constantly resisted, regardless of how attractive and stimulating the enemy makes them. The enemy's goal is to kill, steal, and destroy (John 10:10). Jawanza Kunjufu believes, as I do, that "The greatest problem facing Black America is not racism, economics, or fatherlessness, but the lack of a personal relationship

---

36. Jawanza Kunjufu, *State of Emergency We Must Save African American Males*, (Chicago: IL: African American Images, 2001), 148.

37. Quote cited from www.brainyquotes.com 134846.

with Jesus Christ."[38] To struggle and have victory over the forces in the black community, black people, as well as others, must have a relationship with Jesus Christ. Jesus Christ said, "I am the vine; you are the branches. If you remain in me and I in you, you will bear much fruit; apart from me you can do nothing" (John 5:15).

The problems in the black community cannot be solved without Jesus Christ because there are dark forces that only Jesus Christ can conquer. The church, government, and other social institutions can relieve some of the symptoms, but only Jesus Christ can cure the cause. It is impossible to fight dark spiritual forces without the Conqueror of death and the grave. The enemy is far more powerful and intelligent than the black community, but with Christ, black people are more than conquerors (Romans 8:37). Nevertheless, the black community must watch out for the schemes of Satan, the devil. Satan knows the most effective way to destroy the family, Black or White, is to separate the man from God. A man separated from God is powerless. A man separated from God is dangerous. He lives to satisfy the flesh and not the spirit. A man separated from God is a man who would leave his children. The demon that is driving fatherlessness is not racism; just ask White men. The demon driving fatherlessness is not a change in the economy; just ask all the gainfully employed men who are not taking care of their children. The demon driving fatherlessness is a separation between God and man. Satan knows that when you save a man, you save a family.[39]

It grieves the heart of God to see how broken, fragmented, and chaotic the black family and community have become. This problem is not unique to the black community; it is ubiquitous across ethnic communities. But, due to historical and contemporary racism and oppression that have caused a deficient of power in the black community, the impact is more calamitous. Satan is having a field day in destroying families, marriages, and young black men. Unless the black churches, colleges, universities, and other black organizations come together and put problem-solving programs in place to combat the social and economic crisis the black community is in, there might be a point of no return. There are a few organizations and programs doing their best to combat the problem, but more needs to be done, and more people

---

38. Jawanza Kunjufu, *State of Emergency We Must Save African American Males*, 154.
39. Ibid., 154–155.

need to get involved. It is my firm conviction that once all the loose ends of black social, economic, spiritual, intellectual, and professional acuity come together, black people can come out of their long night of oppression. The enemy knows that once black people come together as Marcus Garvey said years ago, with "One Aim! One God! One Destiny," the power of oppression can no longer hold them captive. "If we must have justice, we must be strong; if we must be strong, we must come together; if we must come together, we can only do so through the system of organization."[40]

Black America cannot expect others to invest resources in the black community more than they are willing to do themselves. If black people love themselves enough, that love will manifest itself in the black family and the black community. For example, if black parents love their children enough, they would raise them to love themselves, have dignity, and self-respect. They would teach them the importance of education and honoring their God and ancestors. Many black children are coming up not loving themselves because they have been socialized to find love outside of themselves. They are killing themselves because they have not been taught not to take what they cannot give, and that there is divinity in others as it is in themselves. Love of self is one of the major components missing in the black community. Unless black people love themselves, all the money and power in the world won't heal them. The lack of self-love that creates a sick psychology and criminal pathology must be addressed. Amos Wilson makes it plain that seeking the love of others without loving the self does not produce the healing it desperately needs.

> The African American community must resist and overthrow its conditioned addictive need to be "loved" by other ethnic groups who can only "love" it to the extent that they can exploit its commercial and economic potential. Even if their "love" was genuine, the community is in no way obliged to impoverish itself, neglect and abuse its children, literally sacrifice its physical and psychosocial body politic by giving away its wealth in a Faustian bargain with the devil to gain that love. The African American community's dedicated use of its wealth to maintain

---

40. Marcus Garvey, *The Story of Marcus Garvey and the Universal Negro Improvement Association*, E. David Cronon, (Madison, WI: The University of Wisconsin Press, 1955, 1969), 173–174.

the employment, health and welfare of its members and its children, to socially and economically improve itself through the preservation and use its resources as allocated through its own social, cultural, and economic institutions, should have absolutely little to do with permitting Korean and other communities free and full access to its marketplaces, only to economically exploit it while smiling pretending to "love" it.[41]

It is not the Koreans' fault; they and others are taking advantage of economic opportunities in the black community. It is because self-love in the black community is not strong enough to close off marketplaces to other ethnic groups who see opportunities to exploit. Carter G. Woodson stated, "The exploiters of the race are not so much at fault as the race itself. If Negroes persist in permitting themselves to be handled in this fashion, they will always find someone at hand to impose upon them. The matter is one which rests largely with Negroes themselves. The race will free itself from exploiters just as soon as it decides to do so. No one can accomplish this task for the race. It must plan and do for itself."[42]

It is my firm belief and faith that the black community can turn their pain into power and their tears into testimonies. The black community must rise and solidify its relationship with God through Christ, restore hope in the village, stabilize the black family, close off its marketplaces to others and take over these economic opportunities themselves, and dislodge from its community those destructive forces that are holding the community captive. First and foremost, the focus must be on rebuilding and stabilizing the black family and community. Marian Wright Edelman stated, ". . . As so much progress has been made, for too many Black children and families, progress is not coming quickly enough or at all . . . We must learn to reweave the rich fabric of community for our children and to re-instill the values and sense of purpose our elders and mentors have always embraced . . . A massive new movement must well up from every nook, cranny, and place in our community involving millions of parents; religious, civic, educational, business and political leaders; and youth themselves. This movement must insist on treating all children fairly and making sure every child receives a Healthy Start, a

---

41. Amos Wilson, *Blueprint For Black Power A Moral, Political, And Economic Imperative for the Twenty-First Century*, 323.

42. Carter G. Woodson, *The Miseducation of the Negro*, 117.

Head Start, a Fair Start, a Safe Start, and a Moral Start in life and successful passage to adulthood with the help of caring families and communities."[43]

There is no doubt that the black community can transform itself as long as hope remains. Without hope, dreams to overcome oppression are dead. Racism and oppression are limiters but not ultimately prohibitors. They are human constructs that can be reconstructed out of existence. Paulo Freire stated, "The dehumanization resulting from an unjust order is not a cause for despair but for hope, leading to the incessant pursuit of the humanity denied by injustice."[44] Another great proponent of liberation, Cornel West, stated, "For as long as hope remains and meaning is preserved, the possibility of overcoming oppression stays alive. The self-fulfilling prophecy of the nihilistic threat is that without hope can be no future, that without meaning, there can be no struggle."[45]

What the black community desperately needs is hope. Black people believing in themselves and doing the work to redeem their communities despite insurmountable odds are paramount. Like Nehemiah, who saw a great problem affecting his people and community and challenged them to rise, the scripture says, "They replied, "Let us start rebuilding." So they began this good work" (Nehemiah 2:18). Nehemiah and the people were successful, despite opposition, because "The people had a mind to work" (Nehemiah 4:6). Think what could happen if the leaders and the black community had a mind to work to rebuild what has been torn down.

Conditions don't have to remain the same. Black families can be reformed. Marcus Garvey knew the time would come when black people would show the world again the greatness within them. What Garvey said years ago, black people must never forget going forward. "Be as proud of your race today as our fathers were in days of yore. We have a beautiful history, and we shall create another in the future that will astonish the world."[46] If only black people knew the greatness they come from and the greatness within them, they would love themselves and immediately stop self-annihilation and noncooperation with any genocide efforts against them and

---

43. Marian Wright Edelman, "What We Can Do," in Tavis Smiley, Ed., *How to Make Black America Better: Leading African Americans Speak Out* (New York: Doubleday, 2001), 121.

44. Paulo Freire, *Pedagogy of the Oppressed* (New York: The Continuum Publishing Company, 1999), 72–73.

45. Cornel West, *Race Matters* (New York: Vintage Books, 1993), 23.

46. Marcus Garvey, *The Story of Marcus Garvey and the Universal Negro Improvement Association*, 174.

their children. The future of the black community depends on their hope, their love for themselves, and their willingness to do the necessary work to rebuild their families and communities into a socioeconomic power. This work largely rests on the shoulders of black men. God put the responsibility of the family in the hands of the male, and this is why the black family is weak, because the enemy has targeted the black male for destruction, and many black males are unconsciously cooperating with the enemy. God has targeted the black male for life and life more abundantly, but too many black males are not cooperating with their Creator in the process of this more abundant life. Therefore, the black family and the black community are suffering as a result. Myles Monroe made this very cogent observation:

> If you want to destroy a building, do you break a window? No, you can break the window, but the building will stay intact. Can you knock a building into rubble by pulling a plank from the wall? No. Can you do it by tearing the roof off? No, that won't do it either. The only way you can effectively destroy a building is by wrecking its foundation, and the foundation of mankind's family is the first made human—the male—man. So if the foundation is faulty, the rest of the house will come tumbling down. Millions of women have suffered because Satan has always known that the male was the secret to the home. That's why the devil will try to keep the husband away from his wife. He will send the husband off or tempt him to abandon his wife and family. Why? Because as long as the male is not in place, the house is in despair. The mismanagement of the male factor is the source of our family crisis.[47]

In the 21st Century, black people must concentrate on repairing and healing the black family while struggling against blocked opportunities to become a socioeconomic people of power. Blacks must look to themselves to save their families and children. "Blacks must stop expecting government, integration, remediation, and the like to do for their children what they should do for themselves. The government and whites know no more about how to socialize or educate your child than you do. If our children are to be "saved" in the full sense of the word, then there must come about

---

47. Myles Munroe, *The Burden of Freedom*, 59–60.

a complete cultural revolution in the black community. New values, standards, attitudes, etc. must become common in the community."[48] When all else fails, family is all we must lean on for support and solace. It is worth saving at all costs. What kept black people going for over 400 years is family. Although the black family was often broken apart in slavery, it still gave blacks an unspoken sense of meaning. Let no one fool you, being connected to a family is the greatest sense of love and support a human being can have in this cold and mean world. God established the family for a purpose, and black people must work hard to save what God has established. It is the most important struggle a people can engage in. The black family is the foundation of the black community, and black people must rise and counter all forces that are at work to destroy what God has established among them. Bishop T. D. Jakes gives profound wisdom concerning the family.

> While the scars are deep and the pain ever-present, it is important that we crawl beyond the past of injustices into the morning light of triumphant possibility. We need to remove the chains that were unlocked decades ago and find a way to build families on foundations strong enough to support future generations. We must educate ourselves, and not only in spite of our past, because of our past, work harder to create and nurture a family unit that will act as a support system and safety net as we endeavor to attain success in every area of life.[49]

Throughout black people's experiences of racism and structural oppression, black families have gone through much suffering and profound stress that may have affected their relationships with family members. Each family member deals with life's challenges in different ways. Nevertheless, they are still family. Family members are not perfect, but they are still family. Family is worth the time and investment in each other. Through love, black people can overcome the flaws, defects, and deficiencies of each family member to maintain their family. God through Christ did not give up on humanity as His family, and therefore, black people must not give up on

---

48. Amos Wilson, *The Developmental Psychology of The Black Child* (New York: Africana Research Publication, 1978), 186.

49. T.D. Jakes, *The Great Investment, Faith, Family, and Finance* (New York: G. P. Putnam's Sons, 2000), 80.

each other as a family. "Family isn't defined only by last names or by blood; it's defined by commitment and by love. It means showing up when they need it most. It means having each other's backs. It means choosing to love each other even on those days when you struggle to like each other. It means never giving up on each other!"[50]

Moreover, it should be a top concern to all blacks in America that our youth are failing in reading and math. It is grossly unacceptable that a large percentage of black children lack proficiency in reading skills. According to the National Assessment of Educational Progress (NAEP), over 80% of black children in the fourth to eighth grade levels are not reading at a proficient level. It is the lowest of any racial group. If black children cannot read, they cannot reason, and if they cannot reason, they cannot reverse the pipeline to prison trajectory they are headed.

At all costs, the black community must come together to address and act on the reading crisis in the black community. Learning how to read is necessary for life. It is the future of a people. A dark vale of ignorance stays over the minds of those who cannot and won't read. Marcus Garvey said, "A race that cannot read is a race that cannot rise."[51] Reading opens up the world of possibilities. It helps the imagination to break free from the limitations and restrictions imposed upon it to discover new possibilities for the future. If black youth cannot read, they deprive themselves of the information and liberation that reading provides.

Frederick Douglass said, "To make a contented slave, you must have a thoughtless one."[52] Crippling illiteracy is a great barrier to black advancement and liberation in the 21st Century. If people cannot read, how can they defend themselves against presuppositions and ideas against them? W.E.B. Dubois stated, "Illiteracy must become a crime." We must treat illiteracy as serious as four stage cancer to the life and progress of the black community. How can Black people know who they are and whose they are unless they know how to read? How can one know what is in contracts if they cannot read? Too many young black men have the athletic ability but no proficiency in reading are easily taken advantage of in contracts.

---

50. *Dave Willis Quotes/ Family quotes,* DaveWillis.org.
51. Marcus Garvey, "Address to the Second UNIA Convention," New York, 1921.
52. Frederick Douglass, *My Bondage and My Freedom* (New York: Miller, Orton and Mulligan, 1968), 320.

The Bible says, "My people are destroyed for a lack of knowledge" Hosea 4:6. To gain knowledge about God, themselves, their history, their greatness, and their potential transformation requires proficient reading. As blacks love sportsmanship and other recreational things, they must equally love reading to counter stereotypes, misinformation, and advance themselves in this technological age. They must get behind black children and youth to help them rise to the greatness within them.

Black America must teach and read itself out of crippling illiteracy. They must demand that their children read at and beyond proficient levels. When the children cannot read, they become embarrassed and stop coming to class and may drop out of school altogether. The community cannot allow this to happen. It takes more than the school to prevent this. The family must be the children's first advocates in learning to read. Black homes must make reading a joy and a chore. The schools need the cooperation of the home and community to save children and youth from the streets, crime, and juvenile delinquency.

There are many things the black community cannot control, and there are many things the black community can control. Helping children and youth to read on a proficient level and beyond is within the black community's control. Diana Greene, CEO of the Children's Literacy Initiative, said, "Reading shouldn't be dreadful. It should be learning, work, and joy. But we can't get there unless we support the whole child and the family. Until we address the root causes—poverty, absenteeism, lack of access— Black students will continue to be left behind."[53] Mack King Carter said, "The message, then, is clear: a brainless man cannot think; a man who cannot think cannot lead; a man who cannot lead has to be led; and if one has to be led, he can be led to lose his wealth."[54]

53. Diana Greene, "Reading the Room: Why Black Kids Need More Than the Norm," by Quintessa Williams, March 24, 2025.

54. Mack King Carter, *A Quest For Freedom: An African American Odyssey* (Four-G Publishers, Inc., 1993), 13–14.

Chapter Three

THE NECESSITY OF ECONOMIC DEVELOPMENT IN THE BLACK COMMUNITY

At the bottom of education, at the bottom of politics, even at the bottom of religion, there must be, for our race, economic independence. —BOOKER T. WASHINGTON

In the 21st century, black people must understand they have in their hands the power to cancel their captivity and dependence on others for their livelihood and future. Black people have the solution to their misery in their own hands. In Exodus 4:2, it says, "Then the Lord said to him, 'What is that in your hand?' 'A staff,' Moses replied." God told Moses, "Raise your staff and stretch out your hand over the sea to divide the water so that the Israelites can go through the sea on dry ground." (Exodus 14:16) God is asking black people the same question today. What is in your hand? To forge a new future, to break free from dependence on Pharaoh, and to become a people of power, black people must realize what they have in their hands. Black people have in their collective hands 2 trillion dollars. This is more than the annual economic output of over 180 countries. Therefore, black people in America don't have a money problem; they have a unity structural problem in maintaining their resources. Jared A. Ball questions the 2 trillion-dollar figure used by many black leaders and black media personalities. He suggests that the amount of buying power of black people is a concoction of business and marketing class interest that was good for business, but does not reflect the true reality of black people. Ball goes on to explain his investigation this way:

> . . . an initial concept of buying power developed by the US government and business elite to manage labor and product costs, as well as the social unrest which often accompanies increases in inequality, was taken by a mid-twentieth-century emerging Black business and media class and turned into marketing tools to procure more corporate advertising dollars for Black-owned and Black-targeted media. From there, the myth has been propelled for decades by an implicit agreement primarily between a White and Black business class whose interests merge in this instance to project a Black material reality that has never existed.
>
> As is the case with the development of the current economic state of affairs, it is true of any change: solutions to economic inequality lie in public policies that determine how wealth is created and how that wealth is distributed. The popular claims that if Black people spent differently, the collective would be better off are the result of propagated myths that deny the role public policy plays in determining societal outcomes. Instead, the myth results in a tendency to ignore policy in favor of personal or community financial habits. The underlying perniciousness of the claim, then, specific in its application to Black America, is that poverty or inequality at all is the result of bad decision-making among the poor. With the least powerful then blamed for their own poverty, little attention needs to be paid to the more difficult struggles around public policy, which are truly what determine the financial success of any community or group.[55]

Though Ball's argument is plausible, there needs to be caution about blaming black people for their powerlessness due to the inappropriateness of their spending habits as a fundamental cause of their socioeconomic

---

55. Jared A. Ball, *The Myth and Propaganda of Black Buying Power*, (eBook) https://doi.org/10.1007/978-3-030-42355-1! (Palgrave Macmillan Publisher, 2020), viii.

predicament. I agree with Ball's assessment on this, and that the amount of 2 trillion may not be accurate, but this still does not negate the fact that, whatever the amount of buying power black people have, they must use it for their full liberation. And, one of the reasons black people are not part-ing Red Seas of powerlessness, poverty, dependency, and oppression is that they don't recognize the collective amount in their hands and what they can do with this collective amount. Of course, economic and social policies are at play to keep black people behind and disenfranchised, but black people must make sure they are not cooperating with the consequences of these unfair policies by the way they spend their money. Black people must be wise with whatever they have in their collective hands because of unfair socioeconomic policies.

God wanted Moses to recognize what was in his hand, and when he did, Moses stretched out his staff, and the Red Sea parted. Moses did not misuse what was in his hand, and when he did, it cost him (Numbers 20:11-12). The misuse of anything can cost us dearly. What I and other black voices are trying to do is get black people to come together and recognize what's in their collective hands. If 2 trillion is an exaggeration, then black voices must correct this and still voice the need for collective economics, whatever the amount. When black people recognize the power of what is in their hands, along with struggling to influence social and economic policies, the Red Sea of powerlessness, poverty, dependency, and oppression will part, and they can cross over to a new reality. Socioeco-nomic power is in the collective hands of black people to write their own emancipation proclamation. Marcus Garvey said, "Before we can properly help people, we have to destroy the old education . . . that teaches them that somebody is keeping them back and that God has forgotten them and that they can't rise because of their color . . . we can only build . . . with faith in ourselves and with self-reliance, believing in our own possibilities, that we can rise to the highest in God's creation."[56] When black people decide to use what is in their collective hands, believe in God and in them-selves, trust themselves, and practice group economics, they can develop an economic infrastructure that will make them respected and competitive as a people.

---

56. Marcus Garvey, *Philosophy and Opinions of Marcus Garvey* (Ravenio Books, 2015), 6.

The goal is to get black people to change the way they spend their money. It is estimated that by 2053, the median net worth of black families will be zero. As of today, many black people are spending themselves into poverty. Ignoring this will be black people's undoing. With a fierce sense of urgency, black people need to recognize the collective power in their hands and invest, own, and control the communities where they live and beyond. The three words black people must constantly think and do are invest, own, and control. Blacks must invest, own, and control their community businesses, industries, and banks to change the trajectory of median net worth from 0% by 2053. To do this, black people must trust and unify. The black dollar only circulates in the black community for less than a day. All other ethnic groups circulate a dollar within a month or more before it leaves their communities. Black people must put the brakes on the black dollar, leaving their community as fast as it does. To put the brakes on the black dollar, black people must build trust among themselves to create an economic infrastructure that keeps the dollar in the community for months before it leaves. This means the black community must intentionally and aggressively find a way to agree with one another to reach common goals, which should be socioeconomic power. Only when black people have power can they stop the power against them. This requires community togetherness and racial solidarity. Martin Luther King, Jr. stated, "We've got to stay together and maintain unity. You know, whenever Pharaoh wanted to prolong the period of slavery in Egypt, he had a favorite formula for doing it. What was that? He kept the slaves fighting among themselves. But whenever the slaves get together, something happens in Pharaoh's court, and he cannot hold the slaves in slavery. When the slaves get together, that's the beginning of getting out of slavery."[57]

For black people to break free from the tentacles of white power, they must create and support black businesses in the community, and those businesses must agree to sell quality goods at fair prices. Black businesses must be competitive enough to keep the black community patronizing their businesses. Once the black community consistently patronizes black businesses, these businesses can lower prices based on the volume of

---

57. Martin Luther King, Jr., *The Radical King*, edited and introduced by Cornel West (Boston, MA: Beacon Press, 2015), 267.

products. Black merchants must do their best to win the loyalty of their black clientele consistently. To do this, "African American businesses can't open late, close early, treat customers rudely, talk on the phone while servicing customers, and have an untidy store that is also understocked."[58] Both the black business owners and customers must treat each other with dignity and respect. This is one of the core values needed to maintain a community and business relationship. Claud Anderson said, "We should seek to reconstruct traditional business communities where businesspersons took pride in the products they sold. Business owners knew their customers were their neighbors, and offered the best products and services. In return, merchants expected customers to remain loyal and shop in stores within their own communities."[59] Cooperation between black business owners and black customers must not be taken for granted. They must both understand the overall goal of black empowerment, which cannot happen without cooperation. The bitterness of racism and discrimination has greatly affected black people, but not to the point that black unity and cooperation are impossible. "Black America has the cultural and economic wherewithal to become a competitive racial group. But successful competition on a global scale will require a new kind of leadership, changes in social behavior patterns, the practice of group economics and politics and a strong sense of community."[60] The key is racial cohesiveness and economic cooperation.

This requires a deep sense of self-love, and this self-love must lead to trusting one another, working with one another, and holding one another accountable in the process of economic development. This process won't happen overnight, but it must happen because the future depends on what happens today. The future is as bright as black people decide to make it today. In his last speech in Memphis, Tennessee, Martin Luther King, Jr. challenged black people to strengthen black institutions.

> We've got to strengthen black institutions. I call upon you to take your money out of the banks downtown and deposit your money in Tri-State

---

58. Jawanza Kunjufu, *Black Economics Solutions for Economic and Community Empowerment* (Chicago, IL: African American Images, 1991), 67.

59. Claud Anderson, *PowerNomics The National Plan to Empower Black America,* (PowerNomics Corporation of America, Inc., 2001), 129.

60. Claud Anderson, *Black Labor White Wealth*, 220.

Bank—we want a "bank-in" movement in Memphis. So go by the savings and loan association. I'm not asking you something that we don't do ourselves at SCLC. Judge [Benjamin] Hooks and others will tell you that we have an account here in the savings and loan association from the Southern Christian Leadership Conference. We're just telling you to follow what we're doing. Put your money there. You have six or seven insurance companies in Memphis. Take out your insurance there. We want to have an "insurance-in." Now, these are some practical things we can do. We begin the process of building a greater economic base . . . I ask you to follow through here.[61]

Martin Luther King understood that unless black people pool their economic resources, they will remain in a state of powerlessness. The last phase of the Civil Rights movement King was involved in was economic justice. Unfortunately, he was assassinated before he could see it through. Deep down inside King, he believed that God had ordained black people to be a free and independent people, but they must come together and make it happen. They must use what they have. Due to the maldistribution of wealth that has put black people behind other ethnic groups, black people must use what they have. Benjamin Mays said, "He who starts behind in the great race of life must forever remain behind or run faster than the man in front."[62]

Although black people are getting a late start due to racism and discrimination, they can reduce the wealth gap. They can eventually become economically independent of white control, but it's going to take a "By any means necessary" mindset. Black people should not despise small beginnings. As Jesus took a lad's lunch of two fish and five loaves of bread and fed thousands, black people must use their lad's lunch of economic cooperation to liberate the black community from hopelessness and powerlessness. "Blacks should capitalize on their potential strengths, beginning with those areas where they are dominant or can control basic resources, such as in the areas of music, entertainment, government municipalities, urban lands and buildings, the approximately $300 billion of annual disposable black income, and the 35-million-strong black consumer market. The hope of

---

61. Martin Luther King, Jr., *The Radical King*, edited and introduced by Cornel West, 271.
62. Benjamin E. Mays, *Quotable Quotes of Benjamin E. Mays* (New York: Vantage Press, 1983), 7.

black empowerment begins at home, in black communities, not in jobs within the 500 major corporations or in white suburbs."[63]

As God ordained the Promised Land to the children of Israel, the same has been ordained for black people, but they must possess it. They must constantly work at it. Blacks must own and control land to build an economic base that provides them with a future of employment and economic security. God said to Moses, "See, I have given you this land. Go in and take possession of the land the Lord swore he would give to your father—to Abraham, Isaac, and Jacob—and to their descendants after them" (Deuteronomy 1:8). The children of Israel must endure the battles, the hardships, the sacrifices, and sometimes the painful process before coming into the Promise Land of liberation and socioeconomic power. God never promised that the process would be easy, but God did promise He would be with His people. The goal of socioeconomic power and liberation must always be the vision and destination of oppressed people in the process of gaining independence from Pharaoh. Unless the oppressed take the necessary steps to let go of Pharaoh, they consign themselves to be under the reign and control of Pharaoh forever.

Despite the prevailing circumstances of restrictive and unfair laws against black people, they must struggle and triumph in what God has ordained for them.

"God is saying that now is the time to roll up our sleeves, dig our wells and take the land. Some of us have crossed over Jordan, but many others are dying in the wilderness with our Bless-Me club membership and lazy lifestyles. Take responsibility for your own destiny."[64] Despite historical resistance to black advancement, it is time for black people to become self-reliant. In the 21st Century, God has given black people a seed of 2 trillion dollars. "He doesn't want that seed back; He wants a forest. He wants you to plant and grow that seed with the ability He gave you. When God gives you something, it always contains more than is apparent. His seeds have the potential to be more than what initially appears. He gives you His seed of potential with the end product in it, and it is the end product—not the seed—that God wants back."[65]

---

63. Claud Anderson, *Black Labor White Wealth*, 220.

64. Myles Monroe, *The Burden of Freedom*, 141.

65. Ibid., 173.

Thus, God wants a forest of socioeconomic development and power in black communities across this nation and beyond to break the cycle of white control, poverty, unemployment, crime, and dependency. Black people have the resources; they have the intelligence; they have the savviness, and they have what it takes to be a people of power. "Much of the wealth that we need is right before our eyes. If we aggregate, we can see it. If we work together, we can acquire it or create it. We are simply blind to our own wealth potential."[66]

Historically, by necessity, black people demonstrated black economic resiliency. They had their own mom and pop stores, hotels, restaurants, meat markets, real estate, banks, loan insurance agencies, etc. Durham, North Carolina and Tulsa, Oklahoma, are prime examples of black people who came together and pooled their resources to own and control black businesses that kept the black dollar in the community for weeks before it went out. Black people have done it before with remarkable success and must do it again. Bill Cosby and Alvin F. Poussaint stated that segregation had its woes and indignities, but it forced black people to rely on themselves:

> For all the woes of segregation, there were some good things to come out of it. One was that it forced us to take care of ourselves. When restaurants, laundries, hotels, theaters, groceries, and clothing stores were segregated, black people opened and ran their own. Black life insurance companies and banks thrived, as well as black funeral homes. African Americans also owned and prospered on family farms. Such successes provided jobs and strength to black economic well-being. They also gave black people that gratifying sense of an interdependent community with people working to help each other.[67]

Black people must show this same resiliency today with greater intentionality. Sadly, blacks lost their sense of community and economic development once desegregation occurred. Much of what gave the black community a sense of self, cultural, and economic power, this unity was

---

66. Claud Anderson, *PowerNomics*, 120.

67. Bill Cosby & Alvin F. Poussaint, MD, *Come On, People, On the Path from Victims to Victors* (Thomas Nelson Publisher, 2007), 37.

lost as an unintended consequence of desegregation. The late Rev. Dr. Mack King Carter said:

> Ladies and gentlemen, boys, and girls, we have been tricked.
> Desegregation means that it is legal to make whites richer. In the
> process the infrastructure of the African American community has been
> dismantled: the family is in disarray; we no longer have discipline in the
> home or the school, the reason being that white parents were not going
> to allow black teachers to disciple their children, so black parents said,
> "If you can't disciple whites you are not going to discipline my children
> either." Black businesses, by and large, have been abdicated; we also lost
> control of the education of our people . . . So desegregation, as it presently
> stands, is a reaffirmation of white power and superiority.[68]

What should have happened is pluralism. Social pluralism is a cultural model in which ethnic groups maintain their distinct selves without losing their individual, cultural, or religious identity. The late William R. Jones states it this way:

> Cultural pluralism is different from both assimilation and integration.
> Like integration, it operates on a two or multi-category model. At
> least two things are regarded as coequal and co-significant. But here
> the similarity ends. Rather than blending the items, pluralism asserts
> that each should retain its distinctive character, its individuality, its
> uniqueness. The end result of pluralism, if we use the culinary metaphor,
> is the cultural smorgasbord, not the stew pot . . . It should be clear by
> now that we do not dehumanize ourselves if we refuse to acknowledge the
> co-equality and co-significance of our point of view. But the argument
> for cultural pluralism is not an argument for black racism; nor is it a call
> for racial separatism . . . Novak perceptively concludes: "To be faithful
> to our vision is not to deny the truth in the vision of others." In a similar
> vein, Oscar Wilde correctly identifies the precise difference between
> authentic pluralism and a despotic assimilationist doctrine. "A red rose,"

---

68. Mack King Carter, *A Quest for Freedom: An African American Odyssey* (Four-G Publishers, Inc., 1993), 23–24.

he insists, "is not selfish because it wants to be a red rose. But it would be horribly selfish if it wanted all other flowers in the garden to be both red and roses." To summarize . . . is an attempt to establish the coequality or different cultural perspective—not the superiority of a black one.[69]

Had cultural pluralism been the goal in America, black people would not have lost so much of who they are as a people. But, due to integration, they lost their self-sufficiency and group unity and are worse off for it. Black America must find a way to regain what they have lost because what does it matter to have so-called integration and your community is now in social and economic devastation? Black communities are suffering from the lack of being a community like they used to be when they supported and depended on one another. The lack of community economics has made them poorer and weaker as a black people. "This continuing preoccupation with whites in general, and integration in particular, has been destructive for the black community in many areas of functioning. For such preoccupation has had the effect of blacks neglecting to use their own economic, educational, and organizational resources efficiently."[70]

Two trillion dollars go through black people's collective hands, dispelling any thought that black people don't have money. The problem is group unity. Collectively, black people are very rich. If they were a nation to themselves, they would be the ninth or tenth richest nation on earth. However, the reason black people don't benefit from the 2 trillion dollars going through their collective hands is not only a system that marginalizes them, but a learned distrust of themselves. This distrust was created in slavery to keep the slaves on the plantation. The house, field, barn, and garden slaves were taught to distrust one another, making it difficult to devise a liberation plan to liberate themselves from the situation and circumstances created by the oppressor.

When people have been oppressed, they learn to distrust their brothers out of a sense of survival. The spirit of oppression and slavery also produces jealousy, distrust, suspicion and hate. When you are oppressed, all you want to do is make it through the day. You'll use anybody to get ahead

---

69. William R. Jones, Unpublished Lecture, "The Arts In The Community: Toward A Deeper Understanding of Black Aesthetics," *Religious and Philosophical Consideration,* 9–10.

70. Amos Wilson, *The Developmental Psychology of The Black Child,* 212.

and to survive life's miseries with more comfort. This is why people who have been oppressed usually fight each other. They don't trust one another, especially when one of them starts to move ahead. They are fearful of a power play, so they band together to pull any achiever back down.[71]

Instead of cooperating with themselves, black people are competing with themselves and losing the game of economic power. Black people must work on regaining their trust. Trustworthiness must be recaptured because if people don't trust themselves, they won't do business with themselves. Economic development is based upon how people relate to one another, and if black people don't relate well with one another, how can they ever free themselves from the socioeconomic dependency of other racial groups? Black people must resurrect trust, race solidarity, and self-reliance to thrive in the 21st Century. Practicing trustworthiness among themselves is key to building and controlling an economic infrastructure in the black community. Amos Wilson stated:

> If I've got money, I can help you, but if I distrust you, I won't help you, and you may not make it. It's not the absence of money . . . it's the presence of mistrust. If I will not cooperate, if you cannot rely on me, then we cannot have an economic system, even though we may have money. In other words, a people must trust, be reliable, be dependable, and have respect for each other if they are to develop a viable economic system. When they have those kinds of relationships, they have a social system, and they can build and they grow economically. Suspiciousness and other negatives are implanted in the collective Black personality so that Afrikan people cannot challenge European people, even though we are a majority of the people on this Earth, and we live over the riches of this Earth.[72]

Therefore, black people must make an assertive effort to learn and understand why they distrust one another. Once they understand the source of this distrust, they must unlearn it to unravel the devastating effects this distrust is causing them. In fact, unlearning everything the

---

71. Myles Monroe, *The Burden of Freedom*, 112–113.
72. Amos Wilson, *The Falsification of Afrikan Consciousness*, 45.

oppressor has taught the oppressed is key to their total liberation. Unless the distrust is confronted, understood, and overcome, it will be difficult—if not impossible—for black people to build and control their own economic infrastructure because economics is based upon trust. Unless trust is reestablished among black people, their collective economic power will go to other ethnic groups to enrich them while continuing to impoverish themselves. Poverty and crime will be the constant companions in the black community because there are no jobs and opportunities to offset this phenomenon. Black youth are caught in this crisis, and many of them will perish—because at their disposal are those things to bring about their elimination, not their liberation.

Black people must unite to create a better future for themselves. Economic power is in the hands of black people to create opportunities to compete globally. They don't have to position themselves to always look for government handouts. Black people have the resources to invest in themselves. They need to harness this economic power to lift themselves from the crippling legacy of white power. Having power can prevent black people from being enslaved again; power can prevent them from being at the social and economic mercy of others. Frederick Douglass said, "A [people] without [power are] without the essential dignity of humanity. Human nature is so constituted that it cannot honor a helpless [people], although it can pity [them]; and even this it cannot do long, if the signs of power do not arise."[73] Unless black people invest in themselves to gain power, they are committing economic suicide.

Albert B. Cleage understood that the uplift of black people cannot happen without power. "We must get power if we are to participate in a power struggle. You cannot get down on your knees and beg the man, "Please give me equality. Please give me freedom. You will never get it. Our basic struggle, then, is to get some kind of power. We must not be ashamed of power. We must mobilize the entire black community to secure political and economic power. Without power, we are helpless and psychologically sick."[74] The goal is to have the power to counter the power against the poor and the oppressed. Attending church, singing, praying, and shouting are

---

73. Frederick Douglass, *My Bondage and My Freedom*, in Autobiographies (New York: Library of America, 1994), 286.

74. Albert B. Cleage, *The Black Messiah* (Trenton, NJ: Africa World Press, Inc., 1989), 197.

part of worship, but when this is over, black people still need to organize for power.

John Yancy Odom, printed in his book *Saving Black America: An Economic Plan for Civil Rights*, a message his father gave back in 1954, is worth black people's consideration. Using the parable of the five wise and foolish virgins, Rev. Corey Franklin Odom, Sr., gave this wise advice to black people:

> There is no country in the entire world that affords the human race better opportunities for the creation and possession of utilities than does America. Despite the fact that there are limitations placed upon our once enslaved group, all are at liberty to produce and possess more . . . The plea "Give us of your oil" most often comes from those of our group who engage in predatory activities—who become the very personification of the foolish virgins, who, when their lamps were going out, to keep from being in total darkness, assumed the roles of mortified mendicants, pleading "Give us of your oil . . ." Yet we beg, "Give us of your oil." No wonder other groups are telling us, "Not so. With the progress you have made, do for yourselves." As individuals, we do fairly well, but as a group, we are to be pitied. We ought to stop complaining until we get our heads, senses, and pocketbooks together . . . We cannot say that we do not have the money, because we do. We throw away enough money in every community every month to put up a thriving business. We are just foolish like those virgins were—sleeping, to wake up too late . . . The herald has already sounded the alarm for us—"go and buy for ourselves." If we buy for ourselves and from ourselves, it will make more jobs for ourselves, and we can better help ourselves.[75]

Black people must do for themselves because soon the government and other ethnic groups will tell them in no uncertain terms, "Get your own oil!" The parable of the ten virgins told by Jesus is challenging black people to do for themselves and stop the great outflow of their resources needed to own and control their own oil businesses. Any economist can tell you

---

75. Rev. Corey Franklin Odom, Sr. cited from John Yancy Odom, *Saving Black America An Economic Plan For Civil Rights* (Chicago, IL: African American Images, 2001), 167–170.

that a people whose flow of money and resources is constantly going out without being recycled many times over will "Ultimately suffer social and economic dysfunctionality and disorganization as a result thereof." This will also create "Breakdowns in social civility, law and order, increases in criminality, family disruptions, drug addiction, disease and death, and a host of other politicoeconomic sociopsychological problems."[76] The black community must stop the outflow of its money and resources, or otherwise have an economic meltdown in a few years. Amos Wilson gave this cogent response:

> The reversal of Black [underclass] deterioration, economic decline and collapse requires that it must, in no uncertain terms, capture and control its economic infrastructure. [It] must eject foreign and immigrant owners and controllers of its internal economy from its midst. It must retard its capital flow outward, retard the outflow of its human resources and circulate those resources within its borders as many times as possible before they flow out. In addition, the [black] community must at least balance its trade imbalance with the larger society, i.e., see that at least as much money flows into the community as flows out. Better yet, the community should establish a trade surplus by earning more from trade with the larger community and the world community by selling goods and services to those outside communities and returning, spending, saving, and investing that outside-earned income within its own confines. This requires a deep and abiding sense of ethnic solidarity, organization based on ethnicity and ethnic identification . . .[77]

One thing black people do and do often is march. No doubt, marching has its place in bringing attention to the issues people are marching for. But, marching cannot create money nor build an economic infrastructure that creates generational wealth. This comes from economic cooperative strategic planning and implementation. Moreover, what is more important to the black community than having the power to stop the oppressive power against them and their future well-being? Therefore, there must be a

---

76. Amos Wilson, *Blueprint for Black Power, A Moral, Political and Economic Imperative for the Twenty-First Century* (New York: Afrikan World InfoSystems, 1998), 508.

77. Ibid., p.441.

new kind of march; march black dollars back into the black communities across this nation to lift themselves out of their powerlessness. Tony Brown stated, "Wherever you spend your money is where you create a job. If you live in Harlem and spend your money in Chicago, you create jobs for people in Chicago. If you are Black and the businesses are run by people who are not Black, then those people come in at 9:00 a.m., leave at 5:00 p.m. and take the wealth to the communities in which they live."[78]

Consequently, black people are doing themselves a disservice when they don't spend money in their own community. To achieve black power, it must not just be a slogan used as it was in the 60s; it must be a way of life and practice for black people in the 21st century and beyond. Chancellor Williams said, "All talk about "Black Power" is empty until we begin to make Black Power a reality in the only way it can be done, and that is by building, step by step, a race organization so great that it will not only be the voice of a united people but will carry on efficiently an economic development program to assist their advance on all other fronts."[79] Black people must learn from the Jews. They will travel far to do business with Jews because they understand group economics and power. Black people need to practice this same type of solidarity. Claud Anderson said, "It is now time for Black people to create wealth for themselves. The secret to creating wealth is to own and control resources, whether they are natural (land, water, precious minerals and metals), processed (machinery, factories, consumer items, public improvements) or human capital (skilled, literate, labor force). There is no wealth potential in public housing, food stamps, petty crime, drug use, or teenage pregnancy. There is no wealth potential in a job. It is the owner and producer of the job who has wealth potential."[80]

To create wealth and produce jobs within the black community, black people must stop telling young people to get an education and expect other races to give them jobs. Black people must tell young people to pursue an education that equips them to create jobs, goods, and services that meet the needs of the black community and beyond. The goal is to keep the money within the black communities for weeks before it goes out, and

---

78. Tony Brown, cited from John Yancheng Odom, *Saving Black America An Economic Plan For Civil Rights*, 119.

79. Chancellor Williams, *The Destruction Black Civilization Great Issues Of A Race From 4500 B.C. To 2000 A.D.*, 360.

80. Claud Anderson, *PowerNomic*, 121.

position themselves so that dollars from other racial groups can flow in as well. Claud Anderson made another cogent point for black people's consideration:

> We spread approximately 95 percent of our income outside of our community. Only two percent remains in Blacks hands inside the Black community. We typically take that two percent to the local White bank and deposit it in a traditional savings account. It is then out of our control, and we generally cannot even leverage it into personal or business loans . . . The question is frequently asked, "How can so many Whites afford to live so well? The answer is easy. Besides having hundreds of times more wealth than Blacks, they also have the advantage of living off two incomes: one hundred percent of their own money and 95 percent of Black people's money. While whites enjoy the economic power of dual incomes, Black Americans struggle to get by on two percent of their disposable income, which is financially impossible to do without some form of government subsidies.[81]

Something has happened to black people over the years. Many of them no longer have the desire for industry and economy. After the Civil Rights Movement, many black people have given up on industry and businesses in the back community and thought they were getting something better by integrating with the dominate society. With a mass exodus of blacks leaving their own community, it left a giant gaping hole where industry, businesses, and opportunities are nonexistent. When black social and economic pastors and scholars look back, they realize black people have gotten themselves into a new form of slavery. Amos Jones, Jr., described the situation of black people today this way:

> Something has happened to turn around the surge in business and industry among black people . . . a great reversal has occurred. Industry among black people, i.e., the development of commodities out of raw materials, is virtually extinct. Businesses begun toward the end of the 1800s and the beginning of the 1900s have either disappeared or are just holding onto survival by a thread. There is little effort to harness

---

81. Ibid., 143–144.

and control the skills unique to black people and develop the skills into corporate efforts that would yield jobs and financial security, and independence for the people. This truly is a great reversal, for it has thrown black people once again upon white people for security, the provision of jobs, and money. It is a new kind of slavery; but it has been caused by black people's failure to follow through on what had begun by their forbears.[82]

How do black people recapture what their forbears started? Where do black people begin? One place is the black church. It is the institution that blacks own and control. It is the place where our emotional, psychological, educational, social, economic, and spiritual yearnings come together as one. Going back to their roots will serve black people well. To get the message out about the inappropriate spending of black people, their disunity, and the things they are doing to themselves, and offering solutions, not just communicating problems, can help the black community to stem the tide of destruction. Not only must the black church meet the spiritual needs of the black community, but it must also help black people realize the power they hold in their collective hands. As it was stated in my earlier writing, "The black church pooled its resources to buy land, build edifices, and finance social organizations, schools, and other business ventures. This form of cooperation kept the black church independent. The black church understood that racism and discrimination would stand unless the oppressed cooperated economically. Economic independence is key in building institutions that would serve and promote the interests of the oppressed."[83]

For that reason, the black church must take its resources to own and control housing, hotels, grocery stores, fish markets, gas stations, restaurants, pharmacies, laundromats, city commissions, police departments, etc., to not only produce jobs for the black community but also create wealth to send politicians to Washington to advocate on behalf of their interests. Black America must understand the linkage between economics and politics. An aggressive effort should be made to build an economic base

---

82. Amos Jones, Jr., *Paul's Message of Freedom What Does It Mean to the Black Church*, 109.

83. Reginald F. Davis, *The Black Church Relevant or Irrelevant in the 21st Century* (Smyth & Helwys Publishing, Inc., 2010), 22.

within the black community before a political base, and not the other way round. Jawanza Kunjufu stated, "Other races have developed an economic base and have hired politicians to represent and reinforce their economic interests. For some reason, African Americans want to build the political base before the economic foundation."[84]

Correcting past mistakes, black people must come together and practice a model not strange to their past, but often suppressed, and that is cooperative economics. This model is blacks looking to themselves for their needs, goods, services, jobs, and opportunities. It was so successful in the past that W.E.B. Du Bois spoke of its impact among black people.

> The group economy . . . It consists of such a cooperative arrangement of industries and services within the Negro group that the group tends to become a closed economic circle largely independent of the surrounding white world . . . The new Negro businessman caters to colored trade. So far has this gone that today in every city of the United States with a considerable Negro population, the colored group is serving itself with religious ministration, medical care, legal advice, and education of children: to a growing degree with food, houses, books, and newspapers. So extraordinary has been this development that it forms a large and growing part in the economy in the case of fully one-half of the Negroes of the United States, and in the case of something between 50,000 and 100,000 town and city Negroes, representing at least 300,000 persons, the group economy approaches a complete system. To these may be added the bulk of the 200,000 Negro farmers who own their farms. They form a natural group economy and are increasing the score of it in every practical way. This is the . . . way in which the Negro has sought economic salvation.[85]

Since cooperative economics worked for black people then, what is keeping it from working for them now? Black people have a choice. They can choose to work together and thrive, becoming a people of power to be reckoned with, or choose to work individually and eventually be crushed

---

84. Jawanza Kunjufu, *Black Economics Solutions for Economic and Community Empowerment*, 26.
85. W.E.B. DuBois, *W.E.B. DuBois Speaks, Speeches And Addresses 1890-1919*, edited by Dr. Philip S. Foner With A Tribute By Martin Luther King, Jr. (Pathfinder, Publisher, 1970), 152–153.

by their enemies, which they are experiencing today. The fact remains that black people must be informed about black economics, and the church can and should play a significant role in this process. Since there are more churches than businesses in the black community, black people must take advantage of this and use the churches not only for information but also for economic opportunities. "With its audience of millions, the black church would not only be able to pool large amounts of money but could also communicate the need for blacks to become better educated and thriftier. It could also sponsor scholarships; stimulate economic development through developing credit unions, food cooperatives, urban programs, and other enterprises."[86]

Many black churches are doing this, but more are needed to help push the black community towards self-sufficiency. When more black preachers and pastors preach and teach socioeconomic messages to black people, they will begin to believe that God requires this of them and move in that direction. The story from the book of Nehemiah is a prime example of how black leaders and black people can come together to solve a common problem. The people in the book of Nehemiah had a mind to work and rebuild the wall that was torn down. Black people need to rebuild their torn-down economic wall, from which their resources are going out to fuel other groups to move them forward, while the black community is running out of economic fuel that stops them from moving forward. The black community needs more black leaders to help them see their collective problems and their collective power for a collective solution. Amos Wilson offers more wisdom on what the black church and its leaders can do to help the black community move forward.

> Whether you want to recognize it or not, the Church and Religion
> are intimately related to the economic and social structure. So the
> Church is not separate from money and economics by any stretch of
> the imagination. This means that we, as Black people, have the right
> to redefine the Church in ways that advance our interests, not only
> economic interests, but social, political, and many other interests in our
> lives. We need to look at the Church in the context of Afrikan life and

---

86. Claud Anderson, *Black Labor White Wealth*, 201.

see how the Church (without losing its spiritual and ethical mission) can also function to enhance Afrikan economic, social, and political life . . . The Black Church has tremendous value as an economic institution. We have church institutions now creating housing, which means that we can begin to use the Church and it can become an instrument for the Black ownership of its communities, lands and properties. These Churches are nationally organized institutions . . . This means that much more information can be carried through our churches. These churches can build and encourage businesses. If they build businesses across this country, we can then build a national network of Black businesses, which will lay the foundation for Black manufacturing. It doesn't do us any good to manufacture and have no place to sell our products. But when the Church brings its political weight to bear and demands White and other merchants who own supermarkets and other businesses make room for a Black manufactured products, then Black manufactures can get on the shelves of these supermarkets, department stores and other kinds of outlets. When the Church creates shopping malls, buildings and other things, it creates jobs for construction . . . So much could grow out of the Church viewing itself as an economic unit.[87]

Notwithstanding, the black church could also encourage the black community to participate in supporting black credit unions and black banks, which could produce affordable housing, businesses, and other profitable ventures. Some black churches own banks and credit unions to support the community. For example, the Living Word Christian Center, pastored by Bill Winston, has created New Covenant Bank to assist the black community. Concord Baptist Church, pastored by the late Gardner Taylor, started Concord Credit Union in Brooklyn, New York. These and other examples are what black churches could create across the nation. To offset the hundreds of millions of dollars that go into white banks every Monday from black churches, while black owned banks and credit unions are suffering, shows that it is possible to slowly break white control over black communities when black communities support themselves.

---

87. Amos Wilson, *The Falsification of Afrikan Consciousness*, 56–57.

Many of these white owned banks refuse to give loans to members of the black community for various reasons. Jawanza Kunjufu said, "In 1993, under the leadership of Pastor Jonathan Weaver at Mount Nebo A.M.E. Church in Maryland, several pastors came together to create the Collective Banking Group. This group now represents 150 churches. They have been able to assemble $100 million in deposits and have leveraged this with banks to create $250 million in loans. The Collective Banking Group was concerned about the ridiculous reality that Black churches were depositing money into White banks from which their members were not able to secure loans."[88] Supporting black-owned banks and credit unions is one way to recycle black dollars within the community and help lift the black community out of economic powerlessness. Access to capital is key to starting black businesses, creating employment opportunities, and stimulating the black community's economy. It would be difficult, if not impossible, to create and sustain a strong black economy without the support of the black church. Black churches must use their collective resources to create a reciprocity situation in which the black community supports black banks and credit unions, and credit unions and black banks support the black community. Malcolm X firmly believed that black people should control the banking system in their own community.

Although black Christians disagree religiously and theologically with black Muslims, the socioeconomic success of black Muslims cannot be denied by black Christians. Under the leadership of the Honorable Elijah Muhammad and now under the Honorable Louis Farrakhan, they have been able to keep the black dollar in their communities and become a nation within a nation. Their motto is "do for self" and "control your own future and destiny." As a result of this motto, the "Nation owned 15,000 acres of farmland, a newspaper with a circulation of 500,000, several aircraft, a fish import business, restaurants, bakeries and supermarkets."[89] What would happen if black Christians and black Muslims lay aside their religious and theological differences and come together to solve the collective socioeconomic problems of black people? This would be a new lease of liberation for black people. The goal is to get together because

---

88. Jawanza Kunjufu, *Solutions for Black America* (Chicago, IL: African American Images, 2004), 175–176.
89. Cited from Amos N. Wilson, *Blueprint For Black Power*, 581.

oppressors don't care about black people's religious and theological differences. Oppressors only care about maintaining power and control. When black people come together regardless of their differences and work on a common problem posed by a common enemy, no power on earth can stop them from achieving the goal of liberation. When the intersectionality of black life and struggle merge as one, the future of black people will look radically different from what it does today.

Having said this, the black community needs more people like Madam C.J. Walker. As an American entrepreneur, she made her fortune by developing and marketing a line of hair products and cosmetics. She employed some 3000 black men and women, making her the first female self-made millionaire in America. She called her business the Madam C.J. Walker Manufacturing Company. She rose from the washing tub to become a wise businesswoman of great prosperity. Having her own business and employing the black community was Madam C.J. Walker's way of fighting against racism and white supremacy, using economic means as a tool to help in this struggle. She is iconic because she understood the linkage between entrepreneurship and liberation. Unless oppressed people have the means to finance their liberation struggle, they may never break the oppressor's hold over them. Chancellor Williams said:

> The overall picture we present to the world is that of a race of dependent job seekers, ourselves unable to engage in the large-scale production of any of the necessities of life, whether they are the shoes and clothing we wear or the food we eat. Hence, the billions of dollars we spend each year, just in these categories, we eagerly give back to the whites to strengthen their power over us while becoming richer and richer at the same time. Economic development activities are direct survival activities, the means of existence—helping to provide the means of existence. It is as simple as that. The main goals of a great unity movement can never be reached unless the Organization has its own self-generating financial resources to protect, defend, and promote the interests of the race."[90]

---

90. Chancellor Williams, *The Destruction Black Civilization Great Issues Of A Race From 4500 B.C. To 2000*, 344.

Therefore, black people must never make money just for themselves; they must help black communities across this nation to become a people of socioeconomic power. "From this fact comes the opportunity for Blacks to unite and develop a more humane economic system of a new kind of community cooperative, owned and controlled by the people in each community."[91] This is the reason Madam C. J. Walker is such an iconic figure in black history. She said, "I am not merely satisfied in making money for myself, for I am endeavoring to provide employment for hundreds of women of my race . . . I want to say to every Negro woman present, don't sit down and wait for the opportunities to come. Get up and make them!"[92] The black community must get up, throw off their doubts and fears, and involve themselves in community economic development to break their dependency on others and become a people of socioeconomic power. It has been achieved before and must be achieved again for future generations of black people. With the right plan, mental attitude, and collective unity, black people can achieve the impossible.

Victor Hugo said, "Nothing is more powerful than an idea whose time has come." Think what could happen when 45 million black people come together as an economic and social power. Black people's demands would be met: they could bring corporate America to her knees; start their own banks to stop predatory lending and outrageous interest rates; redevelop the educational system with a curriculum that teaches great black history; build their own houses and hospitals. Every basic need and beyond could be met by black people. The world would not only respect black people but hold them in high reverence, as they used to before the construction of racism and its manifestations by the Western world. If only the veil of ignorance could be lifted from the minds of black people, they could see how their disunity maintains their oppression. When black people wake up and realize that nobody can hold back 45 million determined black people who want to be free and independent, their midnight would quickly turn into day. To build empires and dynasties again, as the black ancestors did before them, requires radical black unity and socioeconomic power.

---

91. Ibid., 332.
92. Madam C.J. Walker, https://www.azquotes.com/author/19950-Madam_C_J_Walker.

Chapter Four

BLACK PEOPLE MUST USE MONEY WISELY

Money Drives the Train. —James Davis, Jr.

When the Hebrew slaves marched out of Egypt, they had tons of gold and silver. God had given the slaves favor, and they plundered the Egyptians. God said to Moses, "I will make the Egyptians favorably disposed toward this people, so that when you leave, you will not go empty-handed. Every woman is to ask her neighbor and any woman living in her house for articles of silver and gold and for clothing, which you will put on your sons and daughters. And so you will plunder the Egyptians" (Exodus 3:21-22). Therefore, when the children of Israel left Egypt, they were very rich in gold and silver. This was their reparation for 430 years of slavery in Egypt. God had a plan for His people. He was marching them toward nationhood.

But, due to the fact that they didn't understand nationhood and wealth building as newly released slaves, they wasted the gold in their possession and made a golden calf at the base of the mountain (Exodus 32:1-5). They were taken out of Egypt, but Egypt wasn't taken out of them. They didn't have the mind or the mental attitude to understand nationhood or what was really in their collective possession.

Similarly, black people in America have been in slavery for centuries, and although they are still living among their oppressors, they, like the

Israelites, need to understand what they have in their collective hands. Too much money is being wasted on the golden calf of pleasure and consumerism, not enough on freedom and economic independence. Black people spend too much of their money on cars, fashion, and other depreciating items rather than investing for the future. They live beyond their means and are therefore behind other ethnic groups in capital wealth. Carter G. Woodson said, "It will be very wise for Negroes to concentrate on the wise use of money and the evil results from the misuse of it. In large cities like Washington, Baltimore, Philadelphia, New York, and Chicago, they earn millions and millions every year and throw these vast sums immediately away from trifles which undermine their health, vitiate their morals, and contribute to the undoing of generations of Negroes unborn."[93]

With very limited to no financial literacy, mostly due to racism and discrimination, black people do not fully understand the power of collective economics. They must overcome the learned plantation of division and realize the power in their collective hands. "After centuries of slavery, black people must realize that they need to work toward building generational wealth and learn to invest their money and establish Trust funds for their wealth that can be passed down to future generations . . . Generally speaking, Black people are still living for the moment with a 'to hell with the future' mindset when it comes to money. Too many Black folks tend to only worry about themselves and the money that they have NOW. That way of thinking is crippling and must STOP now!"[94] It must stop now because it stifles black people's efforts to achieve socioeconomic power and their ability to create and pass on wealth to subsequent generations. Amos Jones, Jr. stated:

> While blacks coming out of slavery accumulated houses and land, blacks today are accumulating clothes and cars. The desire for ownership of land has eroded among blacks. What black people like is to drive, not necessarily own, cars: big cars, little cars, any kind of car as long as it is a car. The first thing a young black boy wants is a car; he longs for this more than anything else. There is an obsession among black people for clothes,

---

93. Carter G. Woodson, *Miseducation of the Negro*, 167.

94. Gary A. Johnson, "How Do Black People Spend Their Money?—The Racial Wealth Gap" by Black Men In America.com, June 30, 2021.

television sets, radios, stereo consoles, and other material things that wear out, rot, and decay. Materialism being the end many black people seek, the acquisition of material things is achieved by any means possible.[95]

This is not to say that black people shouldn't have nice things; they should. But things don't build wealth. Wise investments build wealth. The Bible states, "A feast is made for laughter, wine makes life merry, and money is the answer for everything" (Ecclesiastes 10:19). To understand money and its power, black people need to have a comprehensive understanding of the black dollar. According to Webster's dictionary, money is "Something generally accepted as a medium of exchange, a measure of value, or a means of payment." Too many people think that money is evil. Money is neither good nor evil; it is amoral and apolitical. It is only a tool. The Bible never said that money was evil. It actually says, "For the love of money is the root of all evil" (1 Timothy 6:10). Sometimes, the lack of money can lead to all evil because when people become desperate, they might do anything to obtain money. It is the use of money that determines whether it is good or evil. Therefore, money can be used wisely or foolishly.

Boyce Watkins said, "Money, like any other powerful object, can either be incredibly constructive or horrifically destructive. It can ruin families or make people strong. It can liberate, enslave, and do everything in between. You can improve the lives of those you love or ruin important relationships. Money can do many amazing things in a capitalist society. Therefore, understanding, embracing, and controlling the power of money is clearly, without question, an undeniably meaningful part of the movement toward equal rights."[96]

Black people must understand the use of money, especially in a capitalistic society. Misuse of money will not lead to respect and admiration. "To achieve self-sufficiency, blacks must master the principles of capitalism and group economics. The window of opportunity for achieving this goal will pass within the next decade. Civil rights, social rights and integration cannot produce wealth and power."[97] Black people must focus on how money

---

95. Amos Jones, Jr., *Paul's Message of Freedom What Does It Mean to the Black Church*, 106.

96. Boyce Watkins, *Black American Money, How Black Power Can Thrive in a Capitalist Society* (Camille's, NY: Blue Boy Publishing Co., 2009), vii.

97. Claud Anderson, *Black Labor White Wealth*, 187.

can work for them to help navigate them out of the deficient situation they are in. There are other ways to fight racism and inequality. The power of the black dollar for wealth creation is one significant way to fight the power of racism. The goal is to achieve socioeconomic power to prevent dependency on white power and influence. Black people have been fighting for justice and equality for years, but have lacked economic power to achieve it. Socioeconomic power should be the renewed and continued way to fight for justice, equality, and wealth creation. W.E.B. Dubois said, "The buying power of the Negro is the most tremendous force within his reach today."[98] Black people need to finance their own liberation and socioeconomic uplift. Martin Luther King, Jr. stated that black people need to "Straightened up their backs because a man cannot ride your back unless it is bent."[99] This means black people must straighten up their minds, straighten up their resources, and straighten up their relationships with one another, and continue the struggle for freedom and economic independence to reach the Promised Land.

One of the reasons the black community is still plagued with socioeconomic problems is that they are not pooling their resources. Carter G. Woodson said, "At this moment, then, the Negroes must begin to do the very thing they have not been taught that they cannot do. They still have some money, and they have needs to supply. They must begin immediately to pool their earnings and organize industries to participate in supplying social and economic demands."[100] As indicated earlier, many blacks left the black community and took their dollars with them, which further weakened already struggling black communities. They didn't understand community capitalism, though it was working for the people during segregation. Simply put, community capitalism is a for profit, business driven expansion of investment, job creation and economic opportunities, which is desperately needed in black communities. Many black communities are missing out on major untapped business opportunities because they spend too much of their money outside of their group, weakening their strength as a people. Having religion and academic education is fine and necessary,

---

98. Cited from Mislan, C. (2013). An "Obedient Servant.". Journalism History, 39(2), 115–125.

99. Martin Luther King, Jr., "I have Been To the Mountain Top" Speech, Memphis, Tennessee, April, 3, 1968.

100. Carter G. Woodson, *Miseducation of the Negro*, 108.

but where there is no economic development and infrastructure, no one can ever rise from their disenfranchisement.

There needs to be financial literacy within the training of black people's religious and academic education. "Intelligence solves problems and produces money. Money without financial intelligence is money soon gone. Most people fail to realize that in life, it's not how much money you make, it's how much money you keep."[101] The proper use of financial investments could help bring to fruition what black people have been marching and going to jail about for years. Marching for jobs, fair housing, adequate schools, criminal justice reform, etc., is within the grasp of black people, but they must understand community capitalism to achieve it. They must understand investment and wealth creation to help achieve the social justice they have been struggling for years. Of course, it also takes organizing, planning, and public protest, but without capital, it is hard to achieve these goals and sustain them. Madame C. J. Walker said, America doesn't respect anything but money. What our people need is a few millionaires."[102] To have more millionaires, black people must practice sound money management by making smart investments.

Nevertheless, due to historical discriminatory practices that have created an enormous wealth gap between whites and blacks, it is time for black people to make a paradigm shift in their thinking and practices in dealing with money. They can no longer survive enriching others while impoverishing themselves. W.E.B. DuBois said, "What I am about to share, you would do well to write on your heart and place in your purse. Many a ruined man dates his downfall from the day he began buying what he did not need. If you are in debt, part of you belongs to your creditors. To whom you give your money, you give your power."[103] Black people must think in terms of being producers and owners and stop giving their power to build generational wealth to others.

There are areas where black people need to increase their wealth. The first area is homeownership. Real estate is an excellent investment. Buying a house versus renting builds equity, and this equity can be used to

---

101. Robert T. Kiyosaki, *Rich Dad Poor Dad What the Rich Teach Their Kids about Money That the Poor and Middle Class Do Not!* (New York: Warner Business Books, 1997), 56.

102. Madam C.J. Walker, awakenthegreatnesswithin.com, "35 Inspirational Madame C. J. Walker Quotes On Success."

103. WEB DuBois, *The Negro in Business* (Atlanta, GA: Atlanta University Press, 1899), 13.

pay off high-interest credit cards, loans, etc. Renting does not build any equity, nor is it a tax credit like real estate. Real estate appreciates over time, and it usually yields a good profit upon resale. Some black people have invested in rental properties to generate extra income and fund other financial interests. Homeownership may not receive the same property value assessment as whites, but it is a great start in building generational wealth. There are community properties in black neighborhoods across the country that could be purchased, refurbished, and resold or rented. If enough black people buy properties within black communities, the value of those properties could increase over time. It is a missed opportunity for properties to be bought and renovated by other ethnic groups, then sold or rented to blacks within their own communities. Real estate investment is right in plain sight before black people in their communities. They should seize this opportunity and use it to build wealth. "A new era is dawning. Thousands of men and women have made their fortune from ideas that others pass by or dismiss. Just as the bee creates honey from the same flower that the spider saps its poison, some men and women will produce their riches from the most common, trivial ideas that others discard."[104]

Another area where black people should invest their money to build generational wealth is the stock market. The stock market is a risk-taking investment to build wealth over time. With compound interest—money making money over time—black people need to take a second and third look at investing in the stock market. The fear of black people's participation in the stock market is well-founded due to historical racism and economic exclusion. Since the wealth of black people is ten times less than that of their white counterparts, losing money is what black people cannot stomach. Unless black people understand the pros and cons of the stock market, most will not participate. Therefore, black people are missing an opportunity to allow their money to make money for them. They are used to having a savings account, which brings them very little return on their money, and do not understand that they could get greater returns on their money when they invest in the stock market. The stock market is a way for money to work for people instead of for people to work for money.

---

104. Dennis Kimbro, *The Wealth Choice Success Secrets of Black Millionaires* (New York: Palgrave Macmillan, 2013), 5.

"Researchers say increased investment by racial minorities in the stock market, carried through future generations, could help narrow the wealth gap. Toward that end, industry groups are trying to encourage financial planners, who could then draw in potential investors."[105] Also, stories of compound interest that have made people like Warren Buffett rich are not part of the corpus of knowledge passed down to black people.

Due to this deficit in investment information passed down to the black community, Boyce Watkins, who has a Ph.D. in Finance and has started a black business school to educate children and adults, is doing just that. Watkins hopes to help black people overcome their fear of investing in the stock market and close the wealth gap by teaching them about money and investing. He is offering an alternative in financial education that colleges and universities are not teaching. For a very low cost, children and adults can take courses online via YouTube to set the foundation for this intellectual financial giant. To provide this type of education, especially for the very young, gives the next generation a financial literacy advantage that the previous generation did not have. Watkins understands it takes money to achieve things in life, but he is not trying to teach worshipping money. He said, "Wealth is something that can enhance your life in a lot of ways. I'm not trying to sell you on the idea of worshiping money, though, so don't ever think that that's the case. I don't think money is a destination. Money is a channel. Money is a tool to reach more important destinations, which are freedom and happiness. Money gets you the freedom, and freedom gets you the happiness. That's the way it should go."[106]

To break the cycle of dependency, dead-end jobs, and powerlessness, financial literacy is the prerequisite to freedom and independence. Learning stock investment is one of the best ways to create and close the wealth gap. J.D. Smith said, "We have to be equipped with the knowledge to transform the income we make into wealth we can keep. Your money must start working for you if you want to build wealth. Wealth flows through us, not to us. We are constantly transferring money between institutions. We go to school and must take on additional jobs to fund our education and

---

105. Stan Choe AP Business Writer, *ABC News*, "Stocks Are Soaring, And Most Black People are Missing Out," October 12, 2020.

106. Boyce Watkins, *How To Think Like A Millionaire* (CreateSpace Independent Publishing Platform, 2017), 5.

overall living expenses. Money typically goes from our jobs to the education system. And this pattern doesn't stop after graduation. When we get into the workforce, money often flows from our jobs to pay hefty mortgage and student debt payments to keep up with the lifestyles of our colleagues. We need to allocate more money toward investing if we want to build wealth."[107] Therefore, regardless of income, black people must invest in the stock market to build wealth in the 21st century.

Another area where black people should use their money is starting a necessary business. I say necessary business because it is futile to start a business that nobody needs what you are selling. Nor does it make sense to compete in the same business. "For example, a [black] starts a restaurant on a corner and does well. Another [black] observing this prosperity thinks that he can do just as well by opening a similar establishment next door. The inevitable result is that by dividing the trade between himself and his forerunner, he makes it impossible for either one to secure sufficient patronage to continue in business."[108] It doesn't make sense to do the same thing because the outcome when be the same. Black entrepreneurs should identify the community's needs and build their businesses around them, without competing with one another to meet those same needs. Diversity of businesses is wonderful for communities suffering from a deficient of power and resources. But once blacks provide the same business in the community, it causes further division, and the business will eventually fail.

Becoming an entrepreneur is an uphill battle for black people. Not having access to capital like their white counterparts, and misinformation and expectation of failure due to miseducation, black business ownership is a challenge, but not impossible. Carter G. Woodson said, "Miseducated by the oppressor of the race, such Negroes expect the Negro businessman to fail anyhow. They seize, then, upon unfavorable reports, exaggerate the situation, and circulate falsehoods throughout the world to their own undoing . . . The miseducated Negroes, then, stand by saying: 'I told you so. Negroes cannot run business . . . Negro business men have made mistakes, and they are still making them; but the weak link in the chain is that they are not properly supported and do not always grow strong enough

---

107. J.D. Smith, *African American Wealth May Fall to Zero by 2053*, by Charlene Rhinehart, Black Enterprise, July 12, 2019.

108. Carter G. Woodson, *Miseducation of the Negro*, 167.

to pass through a crisis."[109] Woodson and others have pointed out that the black community is part and partial the reason many black businesses don't make it. Starting a black business is the first step, and getting the black community to support it is the next great step. No black business can survive without the support of the black community. Therefore, those who start black businesses should know the odds against them, but should not let those odds stop them, because too much is at stake. Malcolm X challenged black people to go into business for themselves:

> To educate our people into the importance of knowing that when you spend your dollar out of the community in which you live, the community in which you spend your money becomes richer and richer; the community out of which you take your money becomes poorer and poorer. And because these Negroes who have been misled and misguided are breaking their necks to spend their money with the man, the man is becoming richer and richer, and you're becoming poorer and poorer. And then what happens? The community in which you live becomes a slum; it becomes a ghetto. The conditions become rundown. And then you have the audacity to complain about poor housing in a rundown community. Why you run it down yourself when you take your dollars out! And you and I are in a double trap. Because not only do we lose by taking our money someplace else and spending it, when we try and spend our money in our community, we're trapped because we haven't had the sense enough to set up stores and control the businesses of our community. The man who's controlling the stores in our community is a man who doesn't look like we do. He's a man who doesn't even live in the community. So you and I even when we try and spend out money in the block where we live, or the area where we live we're spending it with a man who when the sun goes down takes that basket full of money in another part of the town . . . So our people not only have to be re-educated to the importance of supporting Black business but the Black man himself has to be made aware of the importance of going into business. And once you and I go into business, we own and operate, at least the businesses in our community, what we will be doing is developing a situation

---

109. Ibid., 42.

wherein we will actually be able to create employment for the people in the community. And once you can create some employment in the community where you live, it will eliminate the necessity of you and me having to act ignorantly and disgracefully, boycotting and picketing some [White man] someplace else trying to beg him for a job.[110]

The challenges are great, but there are black-owned businesses that have started and are now very profitable. Starting a black business won't be easy, as many black businesses go out of business for various reasons, but black people must never give up on the idea. It is a way to help fight against black people becoming a permanent underclass. Some wealthy blacks are stepping up to invest in urban communities. They are realizing "To whom much is given, much is required" (Luke 12:48). The black community appreciates wealthy blacks for using their capital and their celebrity to help in the transformation of underserved neighborhoods. For decades, Magic Johnson has invested in retail franchises in underserved inner-city neighborhoods. The LeBron James Foundation has invested in schools, residential developments, and community organizations in his hometown of Akron, Ohio, and beyond. It was wonderful to see billionaire Robert F. Smith pay off millions of black student loan debt to give them a fair economic chance and help lift up the black community. There are others, like Oprah Winfrey and Tyler Perry, who are investing resources in black communities to help them jumpstart their financial success.

It would be wonderful if more black investors could come together to own more franchise fast-food restaurants. Black people, especially young people, buy fast food daily. This would employ the black community, and they could be instrumental in helping provide healthier food choices for the community. Also, since black people love fish, they should get into the fish business and help provide fresh fish for the community. More food chains, drug stores, and other businesses that black people need should go up in the black community to help recycle black dollars many times over before they go out. The land that black people own could be used to grow fresh produce that could meet these needs in the community. Black people should own more hotels and motels because, like others, black people travel

---

110. Malcolm X, '*The Ballot or The Bullet*' speech delivered in Detroit on April 12, 1964.

and hold conferences across this nation. These suggested ideas are well within the reach of black people's accomplishments. Before desegregation, black people owned and controlled black businesses in their communities. They must start and support black businesses again to bring themselves out of their long night of injustice and economic disenfranchisement. The struggle in the 21st century must be socioeconomic independence, and with the mind and money that black people possess today, there is no doubt that if they believe it, they can achieve it! Stephanie Lahart gives sound advice about money:

> Many people lack discipline when it comes to saving money. What good is having a bunch of stuff if you're struggling, in debt, or broke most of the time? So many people put up a front like they've got it going on, but they know the truth. They spend all of their money trying to look important, and/or keep up an image. There is a saying, "Fake it until you make it." But knowledge is everything! Educate yourself about money, investing, and saving. I encourage you to start investing in yourself instead of things! Set yourself up for a better future and start making better choices. Building wealth takes time! Have discipline. Save. Stay consistent. Be brave enough to change your spending habits. Be wise! Don't allow money to control you. Strive to have a healthy relationship with money![111]

When black people use their money wisely, whose knows when God may say, "They now understand what's in their hand, I will spoil their oppressors and give it to them as payment for their years of slavery and mistreatment." Genesis 15:14 We don't have to be rocket scientists to learn how to use money wisely. All it takes is a willingness to be trained, discipled, and cooperation. The future shall speak for itself.

---

111. Stephanie Lahart, "Black Wealth Quotes," Goodreads.com.

Chapter Five

BLACK PEOPLE NEED ONE COOPERATIVE NATIONAL PLAN

If you fail to plan, you are planning to fail.
—Benjamin Franklin

Planning is everything. For black people to reach the Promised Land of their aspirations of justice, humanity, dignity, respect, and socioeconomic power and independence, they must create and follow a national plan. This national plan must encompass the breaking of strongholds that their oppressors have had over their minds, resources, and destiny. Without a national plan, black people will continue going in all kinds of directions, never able to come together to reach collective goals. It is mind-boggling why the national black caucus, civil rights leaders, and other black national organizations have not come together to carve out a socioeconomic political national plan specifically for black people. This is not to suggest there aren't any plans because there are, but black people need one national plan to get behind to struggle for and achieve what is needed for them to break the chains holding them. For far too long, black people have been going in different directions to achieve the goal of liberation. When there are unplanned different directions, this leads to division in leadership and follow-ship. But when there is a planned direction, it works to not only build unity but also achieve goals.

There are books written as a national plan for black people. They are basically saying the same things—give or take a few differences in nuances. These works could be merged into one national plan. But, this must take laying aside egos and coming together to take the best ideas from each work and bringing them into one coherent national plan. The major works, and there could be more, are *Where Do We Go From Here Chaos or Community* by Martin Luther King, Jr., *PowerNomics The National Plan to Empower Black America by Claud Anderson; Blueprint For Black Power A Moral, Political and Economic Imperative for the Twenty-First Century* by Amos N. Wilson; *The Destruction of Black Civilization Great Issues Of A Race From 4500 B.C. to 2000 A.D.* by Chancellor Williams; *The Covenant With Black America* by Tavis Smiley; *Solutions for Black America* by Jawanza Kunjufu. These and other works are excellent solution plans, of which black local, state, and national leaders could come together and carve out one plan that may have different parts yet connect to the overall national plan.

The goal here is to engender racial unity to transform the reality of black people in America and possibly around the world. For centuries, oppressors have been successful in keeping black people divided and disorganized to maintain power and control over them for the continued exploitation of their labor. Until black people see for themselves that disunity plays into the hands of their enemies, they will never overcome their oppression and exploitation. Not much can get done when a group is divided against itself. Division is the enemy. Chancellor Williams made a very cogent point that black people must heed before it is too late.

> For the black world, history's Watchman could see no sign of promise, no sign of hope outside of a position of strength which unity alone can provide. But there will never be a real unity without a plan and a program to sustain it. Petty power struggles, bickering and attacking each other are all signs of a death wish as a race. "Which way, then, you still unshackled Blacks?" Six thousand years of their history have answered: Unite or perish . . . Only a largely united people can successfully confront oppressors and, without praying on bended knees, or even pleading,

secure the removal of all shackling chains. The choice is between unity of action in calm, careful thinking and planning the courses of action through one vast organization of millions, either this or ultimate damnation.[112]

When everybody wants to lead, and very few want to follow, getting to the Promised Land of socioeconomic power is all the more difficult. It is going to take unity and cooperation to get black people to produce a different future for themselves and for generations to come. The oppressor has not only created and used the disunity of black people for his gain, but he continues to promote it as long as he continues to get results from it. To stop the oppressor's plan against the oppressed people, the oppressed must stop cooperating with the plan against them. Until black people stop cooperating economically with their oppressors, their nightmare of suffering, death, and sorrow will be their constant companion. Mahatma Gandhi said, "Noncooperation with evil is as much a duty as is cooperation with good."[113] Black people need a plan that will bring them together because there is power in unity. To achieve the kind of socioeconomic political power needed to break from the white power structure, a single, simple, and sustainable plan must be devised and communicated to black people across the United States. This national plan can be the collection of already existing plans condensed into one. Black people and their leaders must come together to agree on a single national plan.

Martin Luther King, Jr. said, "When evil men plot, good men must plan."[114] A counter plan to oppression is necessary to achieve full liberation. It provides direction; facilitates strategies, promotes decision making, minimizes unnecessary risk, reduces waste of time and money, holds people accountable, and helps to achieve objectives. This is the reason black leaders of various disciplines who have a love for black people must come together and draft one agreed-upon national plan that truly liberates black people. When the national plan of black people is in line with the Will and

---

112. Chancellor Williams, *The Destruction of Black Civilization Great Issues of A Race From 4500 B.C. To 2000 A.D.*, 325–326.

113. Mahatma Gandhi, *Statement Before Mr. C.N. Broomfield, I.C. S., District and Sessions Judge, Ahmedad,* 18 March, 1922.

114. Martin Luther King, Jr. *"The Words of Martin Luther King,"* Coretta Scott King (London Collins Found, 1985), 51.

plan of God, the result can be amazing. The oppressed must understand that God desires to work with them. They are collaborators with God in the process of their liberation. Martin Buber, the Jewish philosopher, said, "The fact remains that the creation of this being, man, means that God has made room for a codetermining power, for a starting point for events . . . Does that mean that God cannot redeem the world without man's help? It means that God wills not that He could do that . . . He wills to have need of man . . ."[115] God chooses to work with the oppressed for their liberation, but they must do their part in the process. Part of doing their part is to prayerfully draw up a national plan that black people can get behind to reduce and eventually eliminate barriers against them. God won't do this for the oppressed; they must do this for themselves. When the singing, shouting, and religious ecstasies are finished by black people, without a national plan to follow, they won't be any closer to their full liberation.

Religion must be more than the opiate of the people. It must motivate the oppressed to break from Pharaoh and his systems of manipulation. A major problem of oppressed people is their miseducation. Amos Wilson said, "Their religion, handed down by their oppressors, promises them rescue, a messiah, a Moses, 'pie-in-the-sky'—and thus their revolutionary will is pacified. They wait on the Lord, the tribulation, and are gratified by religious ecstasies. Their oppressors are thus permitted to enjoy heaven-on-earth at their expense."[116] This scenario will continue until black people decide to make a paradigm shift in their thinking and practice.

Black people must accept the harsh reality that there will never be a commitment on the part of the white government or corporations to do right by black people in any significant way. Erik Sherman said, "Without programs specifically targeting people who don't have wealth and need to build it, the country could become even more polarized by wealth inequality. Aside from its obvious inherent issues, such a direction could undermine the economy. If the median wealth of a majority of Americans is zero, there will be little to drive the economy as a whole, and that is a bad prospect for everyone."[117] Consequently, it is imperative without

---

115. Martin Buber, *Hasidism,* New York: Philosophical Library, 1948, cited from in Jones, *Is God A White Racist?,* 187–188.

116. Amos N. Wilson, *The Falsification of Afrikan Consciousness,* 127.

117. Erik Sherman, Senior Contributor of *Forbes,* "Median Wealth Of Black And Latino Families Could Hit Zero By The Middle Of The Century," September 11, 2017.

delay for black people to develop their own national plan because if you don't know where you are going, how are you going to know when you get there! Meandering won't get people to their destination if there is no planned destination to get there. To come out of this American wilderness of powerlessness, miseducation, social annihilation, and economic suffocation, a plan and strategy must be created so that the reality of black people can be far different in a decade than it was a decade ago. Claude Anderson said:

> Decision-making through strategic planning is the wave of the future. The decision to organize and plan is the first step towards acquiring power and increased control over resources. By organizing for self-sufficiency, self-empowerment, and racial accountability, blacks make a conscious decision to both effect and be responsible for their own future. Blacks have paid dearly for entrusting their future to non-blacks. If the lesson has been learned, then it is not too late for blacks to begin leveling the competitive playing field to avoid being locked into a permanent underclass status among racial and ethnic groups in the hyper-competitive decade ahead.[118]

Since black people are very religious, they should draw inspiration from stories in the Bible to motivate them to redeem themselves. One story is in the book of Nehemiah. The great outcome of planning and cooperation, and how it can change people's reality, is worth noting. Nehemiah saw the condition his people were in, and instead of waiting for someone else to solve the problems facing his people, he inspired his people to rise and solve their own problems. The problem was that the wall that would provide protection and help the people to prosper was torn down. Back in Nehemiah's time, a wall was essential for people's protection, but when this wall was torn down, people were vulnerable to all kinds of attacks from enemies. Nehemiah knew the importance of having a wall around his people for them to regroup, restore, and rebuild themselves into a people of power. Before Nehemiah could rebuild the wall, he did an assessment of the problem and quietly gathered people who were impacted by the problem to discuss a solution.

---

118. Claude Anderson, *Black Labor White Wealth, The Search For Power and Economic Justice*, 43.

Notice what Nehemiah said to his people. "You see the trouble we are in: Jerusalem lies in ruins, and its gates have been burned with fire. Come, let us rebuild the wall of Jerusalem, and we will no longer be in disgrace" (Nehemiah 2:17). A plan was devised, and the people got on board to participate in solving their own problem. They first strategized, then prioritized, then organized, and then mobilized the people to participate in their own salvation. Sociologists say whenever people feel they have a stake in something, they are more likely to be constructive rather than destructive. The story goes on to say, "For the people had a mind to work" (Nehemiah 4:6). In days, the wall was rebuilt, and the shame that once identified them was now gone. A plan, a people, and a purpose came together in an amazing way to change the future reality of a people.

Similarly, the walls of the black community are in ruins; the walls of unity, self-worth, self-respect, and community economics are down. There is no economic infrastructure to stabilize black communities. Black families and children are at risk. They are in trouble psychologically, educationally, socially, economically, and spiritually. Does black America see the trouble they are in? If black people don't come together in a hurry and "Face up to the monumental eclipse of hope, the unprecedented collapse of meaning, the incredible disregard for human (especially black) life and property in much of black America,"[119] the nihilistic threat may be black people's undoing. Black people must look to themselves for the answer to their collective problems because, as Martin Luther King, Jr. said, "Whatever affects one directly affects all indirectly. I can never be what I ought to be until you are what you ought to be, and you can never be what you ought to be until I am what I ought to be. This is the interrelated structure of reality."[120]

Black people must practice community again. Those blacks who are doing well should not be satisfied until all blacks are doing well. Like Nehemiah, who went back to help his people in Jerusalem and like Harriet Tubman, who went back south to help her people, blacks who are doing well must go back and help black people who are caught in disadvantage situations beyond their control. This is the reason a national plan is necessary for people in crisis.

---

119. Cornel West, *Race Matters* (New York: Vintage Books, A Division of Random House, Inc., 1993), 19.

120. Martin Luther King, Jr. *Strength To Love* (Philadelphia: Fortress Press, 1963), 70.

Within the national plan for black people, there must be a liberating education. "The so-called modern education, with all its defects, however, does others so much more good than it does the Negro, because it has been worked out in conformity to the needs of those who have enslaved and oppressed weaker peoples."[121] Black people need an education that releases their ingenuity, their innate creative powers, of which they can see opportunities right in their midst. Education should be a tool for liberation not dependency on others outside of themselves. They need an education that pushes them away from thinking of certain work and starting certain businesses as undignified. Carter G. Woodson points out the miseducation and mis-opportunity this creates for black people.

> What Negroes are now being taught does not bring their minds into harmony with life as they must face it . . . The Negro boy sent to college by a mechanic seldom dreams of learning mechanical engineering to build upon the foundation his father has laid, that in years to come he may figure as a contractor or a consulting engineer. The Negro girl who goes to college hardly wants to return to her mother if she is a washerwoman, but this girl should come back with sufficient knowledge of physics and chemistry and business administration to use her mother's work as a nucleus for a modern steam laundry. A white professor of a university recently resigned his position to become rich by running a laundry for Negroes in a Southern city. A Negro college instructor would have considered such a suggestion an insult. The so-called education of Negro college graduates leads them to throw away opportunities that they have and go in quest of those that they do not find.[122]

Not every black person will find opportunities in the black community, but some could be seized upon to help black people break the cycle of unemployment in their community. When black youth get an education, they should go into business because degrees on the walls are wonderful, but they don't pay bills, nor can they put food on the table. There are many blacks with Master's and PhDs who are unemployed. Nothing is more

---

121. Carter G. Woodson, *The Miseducation of the Negro*, xxxii.
122. Ibid., 38–9.

important than for people to learn how to take care of themselves and plan for the future. It is great to get an education, but this education must not lead to dependency on other racial groups for their livelihood. Black people don't need others to guide them in self-sufficiency.

In slavery and before desegregation, let nobody lie to you about the mind and ability of black people. The things black people have invented show that they have never been inferior people. Take a look at all the inventions black people produced in this nation that helped transform America and the world: incandescent lightbulb, X-Ray Spectrometer, Almanac, cataract laser-hack probe, comb, straightening comb, mail box, broom, dust pan, mop, spark plug, street sweeper, railway signal, traffic signal light, ironing board, heart pacemaker, steam engine, folding chair, lawn mower, train alarm, luggage carrier, peanut butter, cosmetics, paint and stain, cooking oil, printer ink, door knob, door stop, refrigerator, guitar, air conditioner, lantern, heating apparatus, clothes dryer, envelope seal, pencil sharper, lemon squeezer, fire extinguisher, fire escape ladder, type writing machine, shoe lasting machine, lawn sprinkler, elevator, oil heater or cooker, horseshoes, scaffold, baby buggy, cellular phone, toilet, helicopter, personal computer, internet, email, etc.

These and many more products came from the minds of black people to make life better not only in this nation but around the world. The education black people need is for them to think for themselves, as these black inventors have done, and work out a liberating plan for them to be self-reliant. Frederick Douglass said:

> In times past, we have been the hewers of wood and drawers of water
> for American society, and we once enjoyed a monopoly in menial
> employments, but this is so no longer. Even these employments are
> rapidly passing away out of our hands. The fact is (every day begins with
> the lesson, and ends with the lesson) that colored men must learn trades,
> must find new employment, new modes of usefulness to society, or that
> they must decay under the pressing wants to which their condition is
> rapidly bringing them. We must become mechanics; we must build as
> well as live in houses; we must make as well as use furniture; we must
> construct bridges as well as pass over them, before we can properly live

or be respected by our fellow men . . . We need workers in iron, clay, and leather . . . We must not only be able to black boots, but to make them.[123]

The same principle is facing black people today. They must do for themselves, produce, own, and control what they have produced because begging and depending on others won't precipitate respect for them in society, and even if others won't respect them, at least they will respect themselves based on what they can produce for themselves.

Another part of the national plan must be the right use of religion. There is no question that black people are a very religious people. But, oftentimes, their religion has not provided the necessary impetus to transform their situation radically. Carter G. Woodson stated that black people's "Religion is merely a loan from the whites who have enslaved and segregated the Negro; and the organization, though largely an independent Negro institution, is dominated by the thought of the oppressors of the race . . . In chameleon-like fashion, the Negro has taken up almost everything religious which has come along instead of thinking for himself."[124] For religion to serve the black community, it must be more than a singing, shouting, and praying exercise; it must be more than an emotional release of pent-up frustration. Religion must lead to radical action, "By which men and women deal critically and creatively with reality and discover how to participate in the transformation of their world."[125]Unless black people use religion as Jesus did, it will only be what Karl Marx called the "Opium of the people." It is simply otherworldly, which does nothing to bring transformation on earth. Jesus reminds us that "God will be done on earth as it is in heaven," and it is God's Will for His people to be free, to be productive, to be good stewards, and to assist the weak and vulnerable on earth.

Another part of the national plan is to encourage black people to constantly vote not only in national elections but in local elections as well. Too many black people only vote in national elections, not understanding that local leaders are needed to assist in facilitating and passing progressive policies that help the socioeconomic uplift of the black community. Voting should

---

123. Frederick Douglass, *Life And Times of Frederick Douglass Written By Himself*, 288.

124. Carter G. Woodson, *Miseducation of the Negro*, 57–58.

125. Richard Shaull, Foreword in Paulo Freire, the *Pedagogy of the Oppressed* (The Continuum Publishing Company, 1999), 16.

never be taken for granted, and if it were not important, why are certain politicians so adamant about making voting more difficult than easier? When oppressors deny or make it difficult to vote, this should be an eye-opener for the oppressed to counter it because the oppressor desires to maintain control over the oppressed. Protecting voting rights along with building wealth are two necessary imperatives for black people in the 21st century. When wealth is built among black people, voting protects that wealth by putting representatives in office who look out for the interests of the voters.

Once black people agree on a national plan and stick with it, it won't be long before they gain the respect of the world, and even if the world's respect doesn't come, to have respect for themselves would be all that matters. Once you respect yourself, you can demand the respect of others. The world has seen how too many young black people disrespect themselves, and this disrespect is reaching new lows. This is due largely to miseducation, lack of opportunities, hopelessness, and powerlessness. But with a national plan, the trend of respect will start upward like never before. Black youth were the hope and salvation of the 1960s, and they must rise up again and become the hope and salvation in this 21st century. Each generation must pay its installment on liberation. They must build on the solid foundation of liberation already laid for them. Chancellor Williams' words of wisdom speak to a new generation of black people.

> The white man as an enemy of Blacks will become less and less a fact, and his hostile or contemptuous attitude will change to more and more respect if and when this race begins to move forward on three fronts: (a) The first is the kind of massive organization the very existence of which means the presence of an organized Power to be reckoned with. (b) The second is a nationwide economic development program, promoted by the unified "race organization" as enterprises of a united people, as distinguished from those of private individuals and corporations. The aims would be the creation of career and general employment opportunities, a national foundation and central banking system to maintain and safeguard the financial resources required to carry on the work of the race—and without which we can only remain a pleading and begging people. (c) Political Action: There is no question about better race relations developing as more and more members of the race register

and vote, and the number of black officials elected to office increases . . . The drive to increase the black vote should go on. The election of Blacks to the office should be accelerated. Still the central questions will demand answers sooner or later: What kind of persons are we electing? . . . Black political power can support, but never replace an organized economic power system within the race itself that gives it the resources to do what has to be done, the only move that will command the respect for Blacks as a people, throughout the world.[126]

There is no question that, despite the setbacks and backpedaling of our local, state, and national leaders in terms of doing right by black people, the future is in the hands of black people today. Black people can either plan for their total liberation or sit back and allow plans for their destruction. Faith points to a brighter future for black people; therefore, motivating them to have the courage to work out their own social, economic, and political plan is key. Though there is much to be in despair about, the faith of the ancestors is "The bottom rail will come to the top," and black people shall no longer be ashamed nor a people of reproach. To speed up this day, black people must follow a national plan that facilitates their total liberation. Total liberation is to live out black lives where they can own and control their own destiny, their own economy, and their own institutions unmolested by racism and oppression. It means to be respected as human beings and come to the economic, social, and political table as an equal and decide in their best interests. Anything less than total liberation is nothing but hollow promises and disguised oppression. With one national plan, black people can decide their own place in the land where their oppressors gave them a place. The answer is with blacks themselves.

W.E.B. Dubois appealed to black people in America and around the world to wake up because their future is at risk. "Africa awake, put on the beautiful robes of Pan-African socialism. You have nothing to lose but your chains! You have a continent to regain! You have freedom and human dignity to attain!"[127] This vision can only be realized when black people have one national and international cooperative plan.

---

126. Chancellor Williams, *The Destruction of Black Civilization Great Issues Of A Race From 4500 B.C. To 2000 A. D.*, 332–333.

127. W.E.B. Dubois, Speeches And Addresses 1920–1963, edited by Dr. Philip S. Foner (Pathfinder, 1970), 315.

Chapter Six

PRACTICE NONVIOLENCE WITH ONE ANOTHER

Mother, mother, mother, there's too many of you crying.
Brother, brother, brother, there's far too many of you dying.
You know we've got to find a way to bring some loving here today, yeah.
—MARVIN GAYE

One of the most disturbing and heartbreaking things to witness is black people fighting and killing each other. For people who share the same history and culture and often engage in the same social and economic struggles, it is mournfully devastating to watch a people destroy themselves. Black on black crime has been and still is a big hindrance to the liberation of black people. It is a phenomenon that black people must deal with if their future is to be radically different from what it is today. Black pathology is depressing, and black people must find a way to resolve their conflict with systemic racism and oppression. The circumstances and situation of structural inequality are factors in black-on-black crime, but it is up to black people to decide not to allow these and other factors to cause them to destroy one another. Understanding institutional racism with all its ugly dimensions is a principal part of understanding the devastating violence in the black communities. Poverty, joblessness, substandard housing conditions, double standards of justice, and discriminatory barriers are all part of a system that fosters black on black crime.

Crime is an American problem, not just a black-on-black phenomenon. Because this American system has created an underclass in which many blacks are trapped, especially young black males, the black communities are experiencing havoc. This underclass is held in place by powerful forces based on systematic racism. When one can see the poverty, joblessness, powerlessness, and alienation, the explosive, violent behavior in the black community can be understood, but must never be accepted. What must be suggested is that they channel their anger through creative means to get rid of the degrading conditions that cause the violent behavior. The violent behavior is the outlet to feel like a human being despite their nonbeing. Frantz Fanon said, "The colonized man will first manifest this aggressiveness which has been deposited in his bones against his own people."[128] Black people taking out their anger and frustration on one another is not the solution to the problems they face. Black on black crime creates another layer of an already devastating situation of powerlessness. Black people must be their brothers and sisters' keepers, not one another's destroyers.

Yes, black lives matter! But how can black people prove that black lives matter when they are killing each other in mounting numbers? Amos Wilson sees this as misplaced aggression.

> The most serious evidence of displaced aggression among blacks is the very high rate of group physical brutality of blacks against blacks, the murder and assault of blacks against blacks. The rates of suicide, alcoholism, drug abuse, and other forms of self-destructive behavior that have been well documented are evidence of displaced aggression. Self-abnegation by blacks, self-hatred and group resentment by blacks indicate a situation where, instead of negative feelings, hatred and hostility and resentment being directed at the responsible party (the whites) or in addition to them being directed that way, they are directed toward the self and the group to which one belongs (the black group).[129]

---

128. Frantz Fanon, *The Wretched of the Earth* (New York: Grove Press, Inc., 1963), 52.
129. Amos Wilson, *The Developmental Psychology of The Black Child*, 210.

Blacks have to find a way to direct their aggression away from themselves by struggling against the conditions to change the culture of violence without killing themselves and undermining their future in the process. It is not an easy engagement, but it must be engaged to bring about transformation. Black people cannot sit back and watch the death of their own race.

There is no doubt that other racial groups destroy themselves. Studies show that whites kill whites, Hispanics kill Hispanics, and Asians kill Asians. Violence is ubiquitous in America. But black people have gone through a particular kind of suffering no other group has in America, and for this reason, they should not become the same hands of those who have lynched, pillaged, and destroyed them. Groups like the Ku Klux Klan and skinheads, and other white supremacists who were known killers of black people have been taken over by blacks themselves. Blacks are doing a better job of destroying themselves than white supremacist groups have ever done. Gun violence that leads to death among black youth is staggering, and at the rate blacks are killing blacks, they will significantly reduce their own population in America. This goes without saying that black people must find a way to practice non-violence among themselves or otherwise self-destruct.

Socioeconomic injustice has always been a part of black people's experience in America, but they didn't destroy themselves like blacks are doing today. If black slaves found a way to survive under the worst conditions without killing themselves, then black people today must find a way not to destroy themselves. What sense does it make to gain freedom and then become enslaved by the culture of violence and death? The progress in this 21st century is determined by how black people decide to deal with themselves, handle their affairs, resolve their conflicts without violence, and create ways to hold one another accountable. No one can do this for the race; they must do this for themselves. Yes, the state and federal government should help in stemming the tide of violence in the black community, but ultimately, black people are responsible for finding ways to work together to pull themselves out of the culture of violence and death. They must turn their attention to figuring out how to rise and cooperate with one another and change the trajectory of their future.

In the 1950s and 1960s, when black people were protesting racism, injustice, and discrimination, they employed the philosophy of nonviolence.

Martin Luther King, Jr. was the proponent of this philosophy par excellent. Some people criticized this approach, but it worked. The civil rights, voting rights, and housing bills were signed into law. Although King was killed by the violence he opposed, look at what he and others accomplished for black people and the nation by employing it. Nonviolence must be revisited, but this time it must be practiced among black people in their relation to one another. The black community can benefit from this approach as it did in the 60s. Black lives matter when black people can demonstrate it among themselves, and if they cannot demonstrate it among themselves, their lives will always be questionable to others. When whites kill blacks, protest breaks out everywhere, but when blacks kill blacks, there is little to no protest at all. The mix messaging speaks volumes. When blacks kill blacks, there should be just as much outrage as there is when whites kill blacks. A life is a life, and those who lose loved ones don't feel any better when that life is taken by a white hand or a black hand. To progress in the 21st century, black people must practice nonviolence among themselves.

To do this, black people must first be taught how to love themselves in a nation that has taught them, through various ways, to hate themselves. The ghost of self-hatred is still operating among black people. When people hate themselves, they don't mind destroying themselves. Due to miseducation and the hiding of black accomplishments, oppressors of the black race have socially, institutionally, educationally, economically, and religiously been successful in driving into the psyche of black people that they are of no significance. Once this sticks in the mind of the oppressed, they will eventually believe it and carry out a program against themselves. It is amazing how this lie has kept black people from uniting to break free from the tentacles of white supremacy to be a thriving people of socioeconomic and political power. To keep black people in a posture of marginalization, look how white politicians are determined not to support critical race theory, especially the work of Nikole Hannah-Jones, who narrates the whole story of the American saga, and how black people were put at a disadvantage because of racism, all the while helping to create a system of democracy. Some governors, like in Virginia, have created a policy against this teaching in public schools.

Furthermore, look at how the government did not support the national voting rights bill to make it easier to vote. Lies are still being told, and there are ongoing efforts to keep the truth buried. If America rejects the truth of her history and present actions, black people must accept the truth because the "Truth will make you free" (John 8:32). To get the ghost of lies out of their minds, black people must be reeducated about themselves, and this reeducation will replace self-hatred with self-love. Self-love leads to self-protection and self-protection to self-preservation. Once people know who they are and the truth about their greatness, they will no longer be ashamed of themselves. The shame of their historical situation will not be on the slaves but on the slave masters. Self-love is the result of such awakening.

Another way to foster non-violence among black people is with music. Studies show that music influences behavior, shapes and reshapes culture, and motives action. Music has and always will influence people and culture. It is an inexplicable expression of culture and vice versa. Whatever a culture values, it finds its expression through music. Since America values military power, it is reflected in its national anthem, "And the rockets' red glare, the bombs bursting in air gave proof through the night that our flag was still there." Music glorifies what we value, and values change over time. Matthew Kondrat said, "Music reflects the cultural characteristics of a society. For example, in America around World War Two, big band music was used to express patriotism. In present-day China, the music listened to reflects the westernization of the country. A Chinese student surveyed said, 'Now many Chinese people listen to music from overseas countries. So, they cherish freedom and a more reasonable education. The culture of a country often changes with the music that they listen to."[130]

Since music can influence the Chinese to desire freedom and better education, as it influenced black people to struggle in America for civil rights and justice, music must not be taken for granted and its influence on people. Belinda Huang said, "Music has the power to culturally, morally, and emotionally influence our society. Thus, the more intentional we become with the sounds, messages, and moods we create and release through our music, the more powerful we will become in making deep positive impacts. We have the mandate and authority as artists and musicians to change the world around us because of the influence we carry, and

---

130. Matthew Kondrat, "Does Culture Affect Music or Does Music Affect Culture?" June 16, 2014, prezioso.com.

that truly makes music something worth dedicating a life to."[131] Having said this, it is a known fact that rap music has influenced a generation of young people, black and white.

However, its negative effect on young black men and women cannot be denied. The lyrics that glorify violence and killings must cease because too many young black men and women are playing out the lyrics on the streets, which often leads them to the morgue. If rap music can influence negatively, it also can influence positively. It is imperative for rappers to change their lyrics to promote non-violence and love among their own people. The impact that rappers could have on the black community and their liberation could be enormous. Rappers don't know how important their music is to the minds of young people. What is asked of rappers and other singers is to use their musical influence to help inspire and shape a new culture for the black community to stop killing themselves and work in unity to better themselves. Just like the music of Marvin Gaye, John Coltrane, and Aretha Franklin, to name a few, influenced the black community in positive ways. Rappers must do the same to help young black men and women to chart a new course through non-violence and creatively deal with their rage through the channel of self-love. Black rage can be channeled through creative ways to help break the cycle of violence and death. Since music influences the sensibilities of human emotion and behavior, black entertainers must use it to help, not hurt, the black community.

Another way to promote nonviolence in the black community is to increase engagement of black men in the community. Black men represent leadership, authority, and wisdom. Disengagement of black men and black fathers has gone on far enough. It is a fact that when black men and black fathers get involved in the lives of young people, violence among them is reduced significantly. In an article by Sarah Keenan in Church Magazines, she describes how rangers decided to separate adult elephants from young male elephants because there was not enough space in the park reserve for the growing elephant population. However, this separation caused a lot of violence and killings in the new park reserve of young male elephants. The rangers found out the problem with the young male elephants:

---

131. Belinda Huang, "What Kind of Impact Does Our Music Really Make on Society?" August 24 2015, blog.sonicbids.com.

Twenty years later, the rangers at the other game reserve began to notice that some of the animals living at the reserve were being injured or killed. When the rangers placed hidden cameras around the reserve to find the culprit, they discovered that it was not poachers who were killing these animals but the juvenile elephants. The young males were abnormally aggressive, terrorizing the other animals in the park and charging humans and tourist vehicles. The rangers ultimately concluded that the cause of the elephants' unusual and troubling behavior was the lack of a role model—in particular, a father. In normal circumstances, the bull elephants would model behavior for their young, helping them understand how an elephant was supposed to act. Without that guidance, the young elephants became violent and uncontrollable . . . In the South African game reserve, the solution to the delinquent elephants was to send in male bull elephants in specially designed trucks. As soon as these males arrived, the younger elephants' violent behavior stopped completely.[132]

Although this is an example in the animal world, the principle is the same in the human world. Young people need models before them to emulate. For example, in Louisiana, a group of black dads came together to stop the violence at Southwood High School in Shreveport. Violence had reached a critical high. But when a few dads decided to come to the high school and patrol the halls, the violence ceased. It started with five dads, and more got involved to have a total of 40 dads. Each takes turns to patrol the school. Young people started going to class, and because these dads decided to step in and stem the violence, they created an atmosphere conducive to learning again. The Dads on Duty program has been so successful that there is hope it will spread across America. Seeing black men and dads in the schools and community is such an inspiration that young people know they must rise to the occasion of expectation.

Michael LaFitte, one of the dads on duty, said, "We are coming out of concern, and out of love . . . I don't care how old you are or what size you are, it's something about seeing a man, a positive male figure, a father, your daddy or whatever you want to call them, at the school. It will make you

---

132. Sarah Keenan, "Elephants, Fathers, and Families," *Church Magazines*, The Church of Jesus Christ of Latter-Day Saints, September 9, 2018.

straighten up and fly right."[133] What these fathers are doing is helping to break the pipeline from school to prison and giving the black community an opportunity to live and chase their dreams. They cannot do this in a violent ridden school and community. Schools may be poor and federal funding may not be fair, but Dads on Duty are showing that black people can make a difference and practice nonviolence among themselves. When black people decide to come together, they can solve problems facing their community.

To further reduce violence among black people is through positive imaging. The way black people are portrayed can induce in them a self-love and respect that leads to nonviolence among themselves. Stereotyping black people for 400 years has led to self-hatred, violence and death among them. Black people must take over their own imaging and not leave it to others. When left to others to portray them to the world, blacks shouldn't be surprised by how the world sees them. When blacks are presented in a negative, criminal, and thuggish way, not only does society reject them, but they also reject themselves. Some people have never met black people, but they draw negative conclusions about them through television, movies, news, radio, and other forms of communication. Imaging informs cognition, and the more negative images people see of themselves, they tend to be afraid of themselves.

There is no wonder blacks don't trust themselves, work with themselves, and quickly kill themselves. When people constantly see what is wrong with them, how can they have self-love? When they destroy themselves, they are destroying what society believes is negative and of no importance. This is the reason many black children still prefer a white doll over a black doll because imaging plays upon their psychological development. Therefore, black churches must get rid of white imaging in their churches, in their educational materials, and in their homes because these images reinforce white supremacy and black inferiority.

Another practice black people must do to promote non-violence among themselves is to speak words that build up, not tear down, one another. Words can hurt and wound or heal and inspire the spirit of people.

---

133. Michael Lafitte, "Dads on Duty: Louisiana, fathers fan out at school to prevent violence, mentor kids," Makenzie Bouncher, *Shreveport Times*, October, 30, 2021, USAtoday.com.

They can affirm or alienate; build or belittle; comfort or criticize; delight or destroy. When blacks use the destructive words that they were called during and after slavery, they inflame hostility among themselves that leads to violence and death. Words that were created during and after slavery to degrade and marginalize a people should not come out of their mouths. Black people must never call each other words that the oppressor has used against them to make them feel less than a human being.

The scripture says, "Life and death are in the power of the tongue" (Proverbs 18:21). Too many black people are using destructive words that are tearing themselves down. Too many black children have been called words that broke their spirits by members of their family and community. Many of these children grow into adulthood angry, bitter, and dangerous; violence is the outcome of such wounded and broken spirits. The more black people speak words of death to one another, death becomes a self-fulfilling prophesy. Black people must speak life to themselves and work in union to pull themselves out of their socioeconomic crisis. Language has power! To transform the violent culture in which many black children and youth are caught, black people must change the way they speak to one another, especially to children. Calling each other names and cursing each other out with words that tear down does not help in the struggle for liberation. Teresa McCarthy made this very cogent observation:

> The fact is that words *do* hurt. They can damage us and leave scars much deeper than those physical wounds that mark the surface of our skin. Verbal abuse can be debilitating to its victims and, considering the source of that abuse, words can shape both who we are and how we see ourselves. ". . . Words hurt, and the pain doesn't always come from overt threats. Verbal abuse is a lot more than name-calling," says Patricia Evans, "Words can be as damaging to the mind as physical blows are to the body. The scars from verbal assaults can last for years" (2003, p. 165). Language inflicts suffering on humankind through two primary avenues of detrimental use: legislative (the language of unjust laws) and personal (the language of unhealthy relationships). Without a doubt, language can be a catalyst for suffering in the public arena of politics and government, specifically in legislation that perpetuates the suffering of the innocent and

legislation that marginalizes certain members of a society or a community. Laws that ignore, or even violate, the most primal of human rights are expressed in language. In this way, language becomes a political tool to inflict suffering on society and, more specifically, on individuals. As Leser might say, "Thoughts dressed like terrorists."[134]

Black people have had enough destructive language inflicted on them down through the years that has wounded their spirits and scarred their souls, making it easy for them to inflict violence on themselves. Once the black community gets a handle on the language they speak to one another, they can reduce and eliminate the violence against themselves. Martin Luther King, Jr.'s words are still relevant to black people in terms of struggling against racist opponents and in terms of dealing with themselves. King said:

> The nonviolent resister is just as strongly opposed to the evil against which he protests as is the person who uses violence. His method is passive or nonaggressive in the sense that he is not physically aggressive toward his opponent. But his mind and emotions are always active, constantly seeking to persuade the opponent that he is mistaken. This method is passively physically but strongly active spiritually; it is nonaggressive physically but dynamically aggressive spiritually . . . The aftermath of nonviolence is the creation of the beloved community, while the aftermath of violence is tragic bitterness . . . This method is that the attack is directed against forces of evil rather than against persons who are caught in those forces. It is evil we are seeking to defeat, not the persons victimized by evil.[135]

Black people can conquer the evil against them, but they must first nonviolently conquer it among themselves. Chancellor Williams says, "The unequal justice system of white America encourages Blacks to commit crimes against Blacks, and even rewards them with lighter sentences

---

134. Teresa McCarthy, "Sticks And Stones: The Healing And Destructive Force of Language, An Exploration of the Theology of Language," Biola University, *Center for Christian Thought*, January 15, 2018.

135. Martin Luther King, Jr., *A Testament Of Hope The Essential Writings of Martin Luther King, Jr.*, edited by James Melvin Washington (San Francisco: Harper & Row, 1986), 7–8.

if convicted. Black life is cheap. Black womanhood is not honored. One may destroy either with both ease and relative protection."[136] Black people must never allow themselves to be played by their enemies. They must love themselves and, out of this love, realize they are their brothers and sisters' keepers in the struggle against structural racism and oppression. One thing is clear: if black people stick together and bear one another's burden and resolve their disagreements nonviolently, they are well on their way to the Promised Land of socioeconomic independence. The goal is to keep their eyes on the prize and not allow distractions to retard their onward struggle to become a people of power and world respect.

Another way black people could honor the legacy of Martin Luther King, Jr, is to practice nonviolence towards themselves. King worked unrelentingly to bring about the beloved community of love, justice, brotherhood, and human dignity through nonviolence. Black people must do the same in their communities across the nation and the world.

King said, "In the nonviolent army, there is room for everyone who wants to join up. There is no color distinction. There is no examination, no pledge, except that, as a soldier in the armies of violence is expected to inspect his carbine and keep it clean, nonviolent soldiers are called upon to examine their greatest weapons: their heart, their conscience, their courage and sense of justice."[137] Black people must examine their hearts and minds before they do violence to one another and further add to an already hurting community. When black people learn how to practice nonviolence with themselves, a new lease on life awaits them.

---

136. Chancellor Williams, *The Destruction of Black Civilization*, 325.

137. Martin Luther King, Jr., *"WHY MARTIN LUTHER KING, JR.'S QUOTES ABOUT NONVIOLENCE ARE RELEVANT"* Cassidy Dyce, BorgenProject.org, March 27, 2018.

Chapter Seven

OVERCOMING THE AMERICAN WALLS OF JERICHO

And the LORD said unto Joshua, See, I have given into thine hand
Jericho, and the king thereof, [and] the mighty men of valor.

—JOSHUA 6:2

Oftentimes, before a people arrive at their Promised Land, they have to
deal with the stubborn facts that there are hindrances that stand in their
way. Some impediments must be acknowledged and dealt with before
people can proceed to their destination. Situations and circumstances that
seem impossible to overcome must be faced because there is no way to get
around them. The children of Israel had to face Jericho. Jericho stands in
the way of their pursuit of the Promised Land. The city was well protected
by a tall, thick fortified wall that was impossible for the children of Israel
to penetrate.

But they had to face Jericho because it was one city that had to be
conquered if the children of Israel were to enter and possess the Promise
Land. God told Joshua, "See, I have given into your hand Jericho, and
the king thereof, and the mighty men of valor." Joshua listened to what
God instructed him to do, and the Jericho walls came tumbling down. It

was through obedience that the Jericho walls fell and the children of Israel pressed on toward the Promised Land. The Jericho walls were faced and conquered.

Like the children of Israel, black people must face their Jericho walls. Jericho walls stand in the way of their advancement; these walls are an obstacle, a hindrance, a barricade, which prevents God's people from entering the promise land of their total liberation. The American Jericho is structural racism and oppression. Its walls are thick and almost impenetrable, but the American Jericho must be faced and conquered. If black people don't face their Jericho, they can never conquer it. They cannot sit back and expect the walls of Jericho to fall flat without their participation. As they pray, they must persist. As they sing, they must struggle. As they preach, they must press toward the mark of total liberation. American Jericho hasn't been easy for black people to conquer because their minds have not been freed from the certification of Caucasianization identification. They still seek approval from their oppressor, not understanding that this approval will never come.

Moses never sought approval from Pharaoh; Joshua never sought approval from Jericho; our modern liberators like Martin Luther King, Jr. and Malcolm X never sought approval from the oppressor to be free. Black people must be their own approval for liberation because expecting it from someone else will never be granted. The walls of the American Jericho can only fall when black people come together and, through obedience to God, see these walls come tumbling down first in their minds and then in their community. Once the American Jericho walls fall flat in the minds of black people, they can start the trend upward and then move toward total liberation. Moses, Joshua, Martin, Malcolm, Mandela, Tubman, and many more all needed God to lead, guide, and empower them to move toward and through their Jericho. Jesus said, "With God all things are possible" (Matthew 19:26).

Overcoming the American Jericho is possible, but to overcome it, the oppressed must not make peace with it. Too many black people have made peace with their Jericho. They have given up the struggle to overcome it. They have stopped reaching for the stars and no longer set their eyes on the prize. They have lost faith in their efforts to transform their situation. They find release through their religion, but their religion does not motivate them to deal with the cause of their situation; therefore, they make peace with it. They don't believe their situation can be transformed. They leave it to God to do for them what they can do for themselves. Making peace with structural racism won't lead to overcoming it, and black religion must not be the opium of the people. Too often, religion has served as counterrevolutionary. Benjamin Mays described how often the oppressed find emotional release through religion, but it doesn't lead them to face and overcome their Jericho.

Certain theological ideas enable Negroes to endure hardship, suffer pain and withstand maladjustment, but . . . do not necessarily motivate them to strive to eliminate the source of the ills they suffer. Since this world is considered a place of temporary abode, many of the Negro masses have inclined to do little or nothing to improve their status here; they have been encouraged to rely on a just God to make amends for all the wrongs they have suffered on earth . . . Believing this about God, the Negro . . . has stood back and suffered much without bitterness, without striking back, and without trying aggressively to realize to the full his needs in the world.[138]

Whenever the oppressed make peace with the status quo, the way things are in this world, they will never overcome their Jericho. Black people should never make peace with racism, injustice, exploitation, and powerlessness. The reason black people and their churches have not overcome their Jericho is that they have made peace with it. They are satisfied with what is instead of what ought to be. They can see how police brutality and killings are taking the lives of black people across this nation, but the great majority of black people have made peace with it. The gains they have made in the American wilderness are treated like it's the promised land because they have made peace with the American Jericho, of which they believe they cannot overcome. And, if people believe they cannot overcome Jericho, they won't. God's people must never make peace with their Jericho walls. They must never make peace with what restricts and hinders them

---

138. Benjamin E. Mays, *The Negro's God* (New York: Atheneum, 1969), 71–72.

from reaching their goals. Black people must never make peace with self-hatred; they must never make peace with other ethnic groups owning businesses in their community while they are suffering from unemployment. They must never make peace with disunity; they must never make peace with destroying themselves because of their oppression. Whatever people must peace with, they will not wage war or struggle against it.

Just think if Moses had made peace with his people being slaves in Egypt. Just think if Abraham Lincoln had made peace with the institution of American slavery. Just think if Frederick Douglass had made peace with being a slave. Just think if Rosa Parks had made peace with segregation in public transportation. Just think if Martin Luther King, Jr. had made peace with discrimination. Just think if Mahatma Gandhi had made peace with oppression in India. What will happen to black children if they make peace with illiteracy, illegitimacy, and high school dropouts? When people make peace with wrong, evil, and injustice, they can never overcome them. They can never enter the Promise Land of life, liberty, and the pursuit of happiness.

Now, how do black people overcome their walls of Jericho? They must first acknowledge the symbolism of a Jericho. They must acknowledge there are economic, social, political and spiritual walls that still exist before them, and that it is their responsibility to overcome them. They must also acknowledge that there are walls they have built among themselves that prevent their access into the Promised Land. There are behaviors, decisions, lifestyles, and abysmal apathy that have prevented them from overcoming Jericho. They talk about walls others have built to restrict and limit them, without acknowledging the walls they have built against themselves. When the oppressed are in denial about the creation of the walls they have erected, they will continue to wander in the wilderness.

Second, black people must acknowledge and believe that the Jericho walls before them cannot come down without God's guidance and power. They have tried to bring down the Jericho walls without God, and they wonder why the walls are still strong and fortified. They wonder with all the money, time, positions, sacrifice, intellectual and scientific efforts they have put into trying to bring down these walls, they are still up. When many blacks become successful, they get caught up in the cares of their success without God, without a sense of community, and find themselves compromising with the oppressor. Many of them stop attending and working with the church to help make it a better agent against oppression. Whatever blacks do and wherever they go, they must realize the walls they confront cannot be conquered without God through Jesus Christ. Jesus said, "Without me you can do nothing" (John 15:5). The walls of Jericho fell because of the power and presence of God and the participation of the children of Israel.

Third, this is the most important of all. Black people must be obedient to God. If the Jericho walls are to fall before them, they must hear and obey God's instructions. God blesses when His people obey. God's blessings overtake them when they are obedient. No wall is too hard for God to break down when His people are obedient. It doesn't matter how long the wall has existed; it is not too hard for God to break down. It doesn't matter how high and fortified the wall is; the power of God can bring it down. The prerequisite for bringing down walls is obedience. When people obey God and keep His commandments, no wall can keep them from entering the Promised Land. Therefore, the key to bringing down the American Jericho walls so that God's people can move into the Promised Land of life, liberty, and joy is strict obedience to God. Regardless of how frustrated, desperate, tired, and angry black people become, obedience to God through Jesus Christ is the key. The same God that brought down the ancient walls of Jericho can also bring down the postmodern walls of racism and oppression.

Fourth, black people must never forget the Lord their God in the land of blessings. There is no doubt that black people have made great strides, but there is also the danger of forgetting the God who has blessed them thus far on their journey. As sure as there is a sun and a moon, black people will get to the Promised Land. They are still on the liberation journey, but held up in the wilderness with the American Jericho walls before them. In time with the participation of black people, God will tear down the walls that are preventing them from getting into the Promised Land. However, here is the warning signal ahead. God cautioned the children of Israel, and the same signal for black America:

> Beware that you do not forget the Lord your God by not keeping His commandments, His judgments, and His statutes which I command

you today, lest—when you have eaten and are full, and have built beautiful houses and dwell in them, and when your herds and your flocks multiply, and your silver and your gold are multiplied, all that you have is multiplied; when your heart is lifted up, and you forget the Lord your God who brought you out of the land of Egypt, from the house of bondage; who led you through that great and terrible wilderness, in which were fiery serpents and scorpions and thirsty land where there was no water; who brought water for you out of the flinty rock; who fed you in the wilderness with mana, which your fathers did not know, that He might humble you and that He might test you, to do you good in the end—then you say in your heart, 'My power and the might of my hand gained me this wealth. And you shall remember the Lord your God, for it is He who gives you power to get wealth, that He may establish His covenant which He swore to your fathers, as it is this day. Then it shall be, if you by any means forget the Lord your God, and follow other gods, and serve them and worship them, I testify against you this day that you shall surely perish. As the nations which the Lord destroys before you, so you shall perish, because you would not be obedient to the voice of the Lord your God" (Deuteronomy 8:11-20).

God saw the danger of prosperity and how this could cause amnesia. Therefore, God warned the children of Israel to pay attention and not allow their blessings to cause them to forget the Lord who delivered them, blessed and protected them. Today, the same warning is given to black America when they finally enter their Promised Land of total liberation and blessings. Don't allow prosperity to become a curse on black people because as sure as they forget the Lord, they will surely perish. The children of Israel forgot the Lord. They ran after the material gods of this world. They allowed prosperity to become their distraction and curse, and they bowed themselves to the gods of pleasure and materialism. The Bible says, "For everything that was written in the past was written to teach us, so that through the endurance taught in the Scriptures and the encouragement they provide, we might have hope" (Romans 15:4).

There is no doubt that black people can get to the Promised Land of their aspirations. They have what it takes to get them there. However, they must move from the delusion that God is going to get them there without their participation, cooperation, and organization. Since, the death of Martin Luther King, Jr. the black community has not come together as it did during the late 50's and 60's. We have been at the mountain of rest long enough. God told Moses, "You have stayed long enough at this mountain" (Deuteronomy 1:6). It is time for black people to move again, unit again, build again, because they have been at the mountain of disorganization, disunity, individualism, complacency, and self-sabotage long enough. The more black people stay at the mountain of the American dream and do not have a vision and plan for themselves to make it a reality, the more they will be oppressed, exploited, criminalized, killed, fill prisons and destroy themselves. They must move from this mountain of delusion that a few think they have arrived when the rest of black people and children are still caught in inner cities and urban areas without hope and without power.

There is nothing wrong with celebrating the passing of civil, voting, and housing rights. Black people have been doing this for over five decades. Celebration reminds us of our past accomplishments and provides mental healing. NAIM AKBAR made this very cogent observation:

> We must learn to comfortably celebrate ourselves. Self-celebration does not necessitate the degradation of others. It does, unapologetically, sing the greatness of our accomplishments and special blessings to the world. It tells each new generation something about the value of the fabric from which they are made. Cultures and institutions put considerable resources into creating images and opportunities to sing the praises of their accomplishments. This process is an essential part of maintaining a free mind, but it becomes even more fundamental in freeing a native mind.[139]

Although I agree with NIAM AKBAR, people should celebrate if they are moving forward toward the Promised Land of socioeconomic independence. Too much is happening to black people to stay at this mountain of dreams and celebration. It is time to go further and achieve more. Celebration is fine if people don't get stuck in celebration complacency. I agree with Chancellor Williams:

---

139. Naim Akbar, *Breaking The Chains of Psychological Slavery*, 37.

The tasks we now face will test this genius of the black race. The Blacks in the Unites States are in the best position as a lead-off example for the rest of the African race. Such a movement would further change the course of history and inspire black youth everywhere, along with their elders, with a new vision, a sense of direction, and the kind of outlook that gives meaning to study as the source of inventions and discoveries. The challenge to Blacks on this continent is to overcome the centuries of their own American version of tribalism and disunity. It is their greatest challenge in this era of perpetual crisis. They will accept it if they have come to understand at last that equal rights and equal justice will never come from appeals to the mighty, and granted as an Act of Grace, but only from their own position of power and influence, which develops from a united people engaged in a great and vast undertaking of their own. If we fail to accept this challenge at this critical turning point in our history, we will have proved ourselves unworthy of having any descendants, and our very names should be forgotten by them-or cursed by the farthest generation. [140]

Black people have within themselves the greatness to once again astonish the world. There is no question that they have greatly suffered for centuries by oppressors, not only in America but also on other continents. Their rise from the bottom of the socioeconomic heap depends on their self-love, self-education, self-determination, group unity, and obedience to their God. There is without doubt that black people hold within their hands and minds the power to cancel their captivity. However, they must do as Jesus told the man at the pool of Bethesda, "Rise, take up your bed and walk!" (John 5:8) Jesus did not come to earth to assist the oppressed in being helpless. He did not come to pity and feel sorry for the oppressed in their paralyzed condition, nor help them to perfect their neurosis and powerlessness. Jesus came to empower! Nowhere in Jesus's ministry do we find him assisting people to remain helpless. Jesus knew that to assist or enable people to remain helpless, they would never develop into the great

---

140. Chancellor Williams, *The Destruction Of Black Civilization, Great Issues Of A Race From 4500-B.C. To 2000 A.D.,* 360.

people they could be for the Kingdom of God. The Kingdom of God is not about helping people remain disadvantaged but helping them to overcome their defects, deficiencies, and disadvantages. Jesus came to empower people to recover from learned helplessness and psychological intimidation, which many oppressed people believe that anything they do doesn't matter. Jesus came to encourage the oppressed to stand on their feet and work to transform their conditions. This is why Martin Luther King, Jr. told black America in his last speech, "To straighten up your backs because a man can't ride your back unless it is bent."[141] Black people must straighten up their backs, straighten up their relations to one another, straighten up their education, straighten up their economics, and straighten up their religion. They cannot change their circumstances until their volition or will align with their desire for freedom and justice.

Jesus asked the paralyzed man, "Do you want to be made whole?" Why would Jesus ask such a question? Shouldn't it be obvious this man wanted to be made whole? Isn't it obvious this man needed assistance? Why ask such a question when you see the man is in need? Jesus asked this question because he knew this man would never get up unless he really wanted to. This is to say, we cannot help people to rise unless they want to rise. We cannot help people to do better unless they want to do better. We cannot help people to be independent unless they want to be independent. Jesus said, "Bless those who hunger and thirst for righteousness, they shall be filled." If they are not hungry and thirsty for something, we cannot shove it down their throats. It doesn't matter how much time and effort we put into making people better; if they don't want it, it won't happen because people have made peace with their condition. America could be free from racism, injustice, immorality, and division, but the nation really doesn't want it. Her will is not really in her creeds.

When Jesus asked this man, "Do you want to be made whole?" We would think this man would immediately say yes! "Yes, I want to be made whole! Yes, I want to get out of this situation! Yes, I am tired of lying here!" But this man said something totally different. He said, "Sir, I have no man when the water is troubled to put me into the pool, but while I am coming

---

141. Martin Luther King, Jr. Speech "I've Been to the Mountain Top," April 3, 1968 at Mason Temple, Memphis, Tennessee.

another steps down before me" (John 5:7). When we don't want to do something, excuses become our first defense. The man had been in his condition so long that he didn't believe his condition could change.

Like the man at the pool, too many black Americans are saying, "Every time we are about to get into the pool of economic, social, political, medical, and educational wholeness, other ethnic groups step in before us." Though this may be true in many instances, black people cannot remain in their powerless state of mind. They cannot keep making excuses like it's the democrats' fault; it's the republicans' fault; it's the schools' fault; it's the churches' fault; it's the parents' fault; it's the immigrants' fault; it's the pastors' fault. Blaming others will not bring about socioeconomic uplift. We have too many black parents who never attend PTA meetings but yet they complain they are not doing enough for our children. We have parents who won't take the time to help children with homework, yet they complain about the achievement gap. We have people who won't read, yet they complain nobody told us. We have people who won't vote, yet they complain about who is in office. Jesus is asking black America as He asked the man at the pool, "Do you want to be made whole? I am not interested in how you got into this situation and who stepped into the pool before you. Do you want to be made whole? If it is really down in your heart; if it is really down in your soul, then take up your bed and walk. Don't give me excuses! Don't sit around waiting for others to do for you when you have the power to do for yourselves. Rise up and walk!" My plea to my people is to rise up and walk! The Jericho wall fell before in human history, and it can fall again. Marcus Garvey said, "Up, you mighty race, accomplish what you will."

In the words of the young poet:

> May this be the day
> We come together.
> Mourning, we come to mend,
> Withered, we come to weather,
> Torn, we come to tend,
> Battered, we come to better.

Tethered by this year of yearning,
We are learning
That though we weren't ready for this,
We have been readied by it.
We steadily vow that no matter
How we are weighed down,
We must always pave a way forward.

This hope is our door, our portal.
Even if we never get back to normal,
Someday we can venture beyond it,
To leave the known and take the first steps.
So let us not return to what was normal,
But reach toward what is next.

What was cursed, we will cure.
What was plagued, we will prove pure.
Where we tend to argue, we will try to agree,
Those fortunes we forswore, now the future we foresee,
Where we weren't aware, we're now awake;
Those moments we missed
Are now these moments we make,
The moments we meet,
And our hearts, once all together beaten,
Now all together beat.

Come, look up with kindness yet,
For even solace can be sourced from sorrow.
We remember, not just for the sake of yesterday,
But to take on tomorrow.

We heed this old spirit,
In a new day's lyric,
In our hearts, we hear it:
For auld lang syne, my dear,

For auld lang syne.
Be bold, sang Time this year,
Be bold, sang Time,
For when you honor yesterday,
Tomorrow ye will find.
Know what we've fought
Need not be forgot nor for none.
It defines us, binds us as one,
Come over, join this day just begun.
For wherever we come together,
We will forever overcome.[142]

142. Amanda Gordon, *"New Day's Lyric,"* Instagram.com, 2022.

Chapter Eight

WE ARE THE ONES WE HAVE BEEN WAITING FOR

The wonder is that so many of us refuse to give in, that we summon the strength to resist society's expectation and discover how truly wonderful-and special-we can be. —Ellis Cose

There is something about black people that the world envies. Is it their strength? Is it the melanin in their skin? Is it because Egypt was the cradle of civilization, and black people are descendants of historical greatness? Is it because the invisible God chose to manifest Himself in His Son out of Africa? Why is it that the western world continues to oppress and use reverse psychology on a people who gave the world civilization? The answer to these questions is they are God's chosen people; the lost sheep of Israel who were brought to the western world to give civilization, agriculture, math, science, religion, morality, governance, and medicine. Their strength and resiliency can only be attributed to the Spirit of God within them that makes them enduring people despite a myriad of opposition against them.

Jeremiah A. Wright, Jr. asked the question years ago concerning black people. What makes you so strong? "No other race was brought to this country in chains. No other race had laws passed making it a crime to teach them to read. No other race had skin color as a determining factor of their servitude and their employability. No other race was hounded and haunted when they wanted to be free. No other race was physically mutilated to identify them as

"

property, not people. No other race was lied to and lied on like the African race. No other race had its names taken away in addition to its language and music. No other race was denied more and deprived of more, treated as badly and treated as less than human. No other race was treated like the Africans were treated, and yet no other race has done so much after starting out with so little, defying all of the odds and breaking all the records."[143]

With this type of dogged strength and endurance, and to still be here and standing is a testament that black people are God's chosen. Many of them may not know their God but their God surly knows them. "The ox knows its master, the donkey its owner's manger, but Israel does not know, my people do not understand." Isaiah 1:3 The truth about who they are is coming to the surface because Jesus said, "For there is nothing hidden that will not be disclosed, and nothing concealed that will not be known or brought out into open." Luke 8:17 Therefore, black people's true history is coming to the light. All the lies, manipulations, deceptions, and hidden facts about them are being exposed to the world, and there is no need for them to despair because their liberation is at hand. All black people need to do is believe they are the ones they have been waiting for, and stick together to achieve their liberation. This solidarity would help to promote black businesses, schools, mentorship, validation, emotional spiritual support, economic and social power to control their destiny.

We now know that desegregation has not worked for the masses of black people. Conditions have worsen for black people since the Civil Right Movement. Looking back in hindsight, black people pinned their hopes and dreams upon the American Pharaoh who never intended to do right about them. Therefore, this is an opportunity for black people to lay aside their divisions, acknowledge the mistakes, and look to God and themselves for the solutions to their collective problem. Cassius said to Brutus in one of the plays of Shakespeare, "Dear Brutus the problem is not in the stars but in ourselves, for every bondman holds within his hand the power to cancel his captivity."[144] Black people have the power to be their own liberators in this world of racial oppression, racism, and terrorism. They have the power to cancer cooperation with oppression, exploitation,

---

143. Jeremiah A. Wright, Jr, *What Makes You So Strong, Sermons of Joy and Strength* (Valley Forge, PA: Judson Press, 1993), 151.

144. William Shakespeare, *Julius Caesar I*, iii, 101.

miseducation, and marginalization. They have the power to create their own liberation agenda.

Of course, they must be prepared for the opposition of the power structure, and not get distracted by the tricks and politics of the American empire. Black people must stay focused on their liberation and not get caught up in the political divisions while the white establishment remains in power. Whenever black people get caught up in what Frederick Douglass called, the "White Man's problem" it does not serve the liberation of the black community. Racism, oppression, white supremacy are in totality the "White man's problem," which has devastated the black community. Black people's time and energy should be on liberating themselves from the "white man's problem," and they cannot do this as long as they subject themselves to the tricks and politics of the American empire.

Black people must understand that while they are sleeping, oppressors are devising ways to keep them oppressed, confused, and divided. This is the reason a strategic plan was put in place during and after slavery to contain them. The plan has been effective to this day. One of many plans is spelled out in the Willie Lynch Speech of 1712:

> Gentlemen . . . I am here to provide a method of controlling your black slaves. I guarantee everyone of you that installed correctly it will control the slave for at least 300 years. . . . I have outlined a number of differences among the slaves and I take these differences and make them bigger. I use fear, mistrust, and envy for control purposes. . . . Take this simple little list of differences and think about them. On the top of my list is age, but it is there only because it starts with the letter A. The second is color or shade. There is intelligence, size, sex, size of plantation, attitude of owners, whether the slave lived in the valley, on the hill, east, west, north, south, has fine or coarse hair or is tall or short.
>
> Now that you have a list of differences, I shall give you an outline of action. But before that I shall assure you that distrust is stronger than trust and envy is stronger than adulation, respect, or admiration.
>
> The black slave, after receiving this indoctrination, shall carry on and become self-refueling and self-generating for hundreds of years, maybe thousands. Don't forget, you must pitch the old black versus the

young black male and the young black male against the old black male. You must use the dark skinned slaves versus the light skinned slaves and the light skinned slaves versus the dark skinned slaves. You must use the female versus the male and the male versus the female. You must also have your servants and overseers distrust all blacks, but it is necessary that your slaves trust and depend on us. They must love, respect, and trust only us.

Gentlemen, these kits are your keys to control. Use them. Have your wives and children use them. Never miss an opportunity. My plan is guaranteed, and the good thing about this plan is that if used intensely for one year, the slaves themselves will remain perpetually distrustful.[145]

Who doubts today this planned strategy to keep black people divided is still working in some form or fashion across the United States and the world? Black people must understand that oppressors are fearful of black unity, and they have think tanks across this nation to study black people in an effort to keep them divided. Unclassified documents of the FBI files reveal that one of their strategies is to "discredit, disrupt and destroy." Whatever actions black people take to free themselves from the oppressive system of racism and marginalization, are viewed as a threat to the disruption of white hegemony and racial hierarchy. Fear keeps oppressors strategizing against the unity of the oppressed.

It is the same fear Pharaoh had while the Israelites were in Egypt. When Pharaoh saw the number of Israelites and their prosperity in Egypt, he said, "Look, the people of the children of Israel are more and mightier than we; come let us deal shrewdly with them, lest they multiply, and it happen, in the event of war, that they also join our enemies and fight against us, and so go up out of the land.' Therefore they set taskmasters over them to afflict them with burdens. And they built for Pharaoh supply cities, Pithom, and Raamses. But, the more they afflicted them, the more they multiplied and grew. And they were in dread of the children of Israel. So the Egyptians made the children of Israel serve with rigor. And they made their lives bitter with hard bondage—in mortar, in brick, and all manner of service in the field. All their service in which they made them serve was with rigor." Exodus 1:9-14 Fear of black unity caused Pharaoh to enslave

---

145. Willie Lynch Speech given on the banks of the James River in 1712.

them to maintain control over them. Since black people are descendants of the Israelites, the same plan has been practiced on them in America.

With this understanding, black people must come to see that unity among them must be a great benefit to cause great fear in the oppressor. This is the reason white supremacy must be advanced and protected at all cost, and there isn't anything black people can do to eliminate the fear of black unity in the American Pharaoh. Power and control over black people was the strategy then as it is now. Black people cannot sacrifice enough, contribute enough, be loyal enough, die enough, patriotic enough, and sweat enough blood and tears to share in the power and resources of the American Pharaoh. Pharaoh may allow a hand few to rise to appease the many, but the mass of black people are denied the same privilege. If black people cannot see that out of all the blood, sweat, and tears, out of all the wars they have fought in to advance the cause of America, out of 250 years of physical slavery, out of being cheated of generational wealth, and the present reality of having their gains rolled back again, then Amos Wilson words rings true, "Black people are living out of their minds."

Living out of their minds is one of the major reasons they are continuing to experience economic disparities, miseducation, joblessness, disunity, and powerlessness. Until black people deal with the trauma of hurt and injury done to their brains created from their long experience with slavery, racism, and oppression, they will not develop the necessary consciousness to achieve liberation. The challenge facing black America is to break the chain of psychological slavery. It cannot be expressed enough the desperate need for psychological emancipation in this 21st century to achieve authentic liberation for a hurt and injured people. Because this psychological healing has not taken place, transgenerational trauma is played out in many places where black people live, work, and worship. Unacknowledged and untreated trauma poses a threat to black liberation, and what is more grievous, many black people don't want to go and get help for their trauma. They don't understand this does not facilitate wholesome relationships but causes alienation. Dr. Da'Mond Holt, a certified traumatologist said, "In a Black family, Black communities, we don't talk about things. We don't go to the doctor, we don't see counselors, we don't go to therapists, we don't like talking about what we issue. So we have a lot of family secrets in Black families. All of that is like a pressure cooker brewing, just waiting for that opportunity for an explosion. And so when we don't heal from our traumas and we allow these things to happen and exacerbate the outcomes for African Americans without the right love, without the right treatment, without the support network and building those types of support networks, can be very maladaptive for our community."[146] Black people must get help for their trauma to help their community achieve liberation goals. Untreated trauma stifles the progress of unity and advancement among black people. Trauma can be healed, but the healing can only come by acknowledging the injury and the willingness to get help. With love, support, and networking, the brain can be healed and the mind can be set free.

My appeal to black people is we are in this liberation struggle together. We share historical commonality of oppression and suffering, and must use this commonality and connection to our benefit. We must build community again to not only take care of socioeconomic deficits of power and miseducation, but to also heal ourselves of the trauma brought on by oppression. There are enough trained counselors, doctors, teachers, economists, etc. among black people to address every area of our collective lives. But, it is going to take releasing the mind from the shackles of oppression to see that the answers to our collective problems are right in our midst. Let us give ourselves a chance to prove that we can love ourselves, support ourselves, heal, and liberate ourselves. We have the power within ourselves to achieve it. In the words of the late Ed Bullins:

> Into your palm I place the ashes,
> Into your palm are the ashes of your people . . .
> Take the ashes of your nation,
> And create the cement to build again.
> Create the spirit to move again.
> Take this soul dust and begin again.[147]

Black people we are the hopes and dreams of the ancestors. Let us take the dust of our ancestors and organize again, build again, achieve again, transform again, produce again, lead, struggle, and liberate again so that generations to come will know that we are the ones we have been waiting for!

---

146. Dr. Da'Mond Holt, interviewed by Mansa Musa, "The Reality of Black Historical Trauma Making Healing A Form of Justice," June 3, 2024, https://therealnews.com.

147. Ed Bullins, *Creation Spell.*

BIBLIOGRAPHY

Books

AKBAR, NAIM, *Breaking The Chains of Psychological Slavery*, Published by Mind Productions & Associates, Tallahassee, Florida, 1996.

Anderson, Carol, *White Rage: The Unspoken Truth of Our Racial Divide*, Bloomsbury Publisher, New York, New York, 2017.

Anderson, Claud, *Black Labor White Wealth, The Search for Power and Economic Justice*, PowerNomics Corporation of America, Publisher, 1994.

————. *PowerNomics: The National Plan to Empower Black America*, PowerNomics Corporation of America, Inc. Publisher, 2001.

Ball, Jared A., *The Myth and Propaganda of Black Buying Power*, Palgrave Macmillan Publisher, 2020.

Bell, Janet Cheatham, Selected and Compiled, *Black Quotation And Some Not So Famous*, Sabayt Publications, Chicago, Illinois, 1986.

Bennett, Jr. Lerone, *The Challenge of Blackness*, Johnson Publishing Company, Chicago, IL, 1972.

Blassingame, John, The Frederick Douglass Papers, series Three, Speeches, Debates, and Interviews, Vol. 3, 1855-63, New Haven: Yale University Press, 1985.

Buber, Martin, *Hasidism*, New York: Philosophical Library, 1948.

Carter, Mack King, *A Quest for Freedom: An African American Odyssey*, Four-G Publishers, Incorporated, 1993.

Cleage, Albert B., *Black Messiah*, Africa World Press, Inc., Trenton, New Jersey, 1989.

Cronon, E. David, *The Story of Marcus Garvey and the Universal Negro Improvement Association*, The University of Wisconsin Press, Madison, Wisconsin, 1955, 1969.

Cosby, Bill & Alvin F. Poussaint, MD, *Come On, People, On the Path from Victims to Victors*, Thomas Nelson Publisher, 2007.

Davis, Reginald F., *Black Church Relevant or Irrelevant in the 21st Century*, Smyth & Helwys Publishing, Inc., 2010.

Drew, Benjamin, Editor, Harriet Tubman, *The Refugee: Or the Narratives of Fugitive Slaves in Canada*, Boston: John P. Jewett and Company, 1856.

Douglass, Frederick, *Bondage and My Freedom*, in Autobiographies, New York: Library of America, 1994.

————. *Life And Times of Frederick Douglass*, Macmillan Publishing Company, New York, New York, 1962.

————. *The Life and Times of Frederick Douglass*, Pathway Press, New York, 1941.

DuBois, W.E.B., *The Negro in Business* (Atlanta, GA: Atlanta University Press, 1899).

————. *DuBois Speaks, Speeches And Addresses 1890–1919*, Edited by Dr. Philip S. Foner With A Tribute By Martin Luther King, Jr., Pathfinder, Publisher, 1970.

————. *The Souls of Black Folk*, New York: Penguin, 1969.

Fanon, Frantz, *The Wretched of the Earth*, Grove Press, Inc., New York, 1963.

Fisher, Louis, *Gandhi His Life and Message for the World*, New American Library, A Signet Key Book, New York, New York, 1954.

Franklin, Robert M., *In The Village Restoring Hope in African American Communities*, Fortress Press, Minneapolis, MN, 2007.

Freire, Paulo, *Pedagogy of the Oppressed*, The Continuum Publishing Company, New York, New York, 1999.

Jakes, T.D. *The Great Investment, Faith, Family, and Finance*, G. P. Putnam's Sons, Publisher, New York, New York, 2000.

Jones, Jr., Amos, *Paul's Message of Freedom: What Does It Mean to the Black Church*, Judson Press, Valley Forge, 1984.

Kimbro, Dennis, *The Wealth Choice Success Secrets of Black Millionaires*, Palgrave Macmillan, New York, New York, 2013.

King, Coretta Scott, *The Words of Martin Luther King*. London Collins Found, 1985.

King, Jr., Martin Luther, *Where Do We Go From Here: Chaos or Community?* New York: Harper and Row, 1967.

————. *Strength To Love*, Fortress Press, Philadelphia, 1963.

Kiyosaki, Robert T., *Rich Dad Poor Dad: What the Rich Teach Their Kids about Money That the Poor and Middle Class Do Not!*, Warner Business Books, New York, New York, 1997.

Kunjufu, Jawanza, *State of Emergency We Must Save African American Males*, African American Images, Publisher, Chicago, Illinois, 2001.

————. *Black Economics Solutions for Economic and Community Empowerment*, African American Images, Chicago, Illinois, 1991.

Mays, Benjamin E., *The Negro's God*, Atheneum, Publisher, New York, 1969.

Mays, Benjamin E., *Quotable Quotes of Benjamin E. Mays*, Vantage Press, New York, 1983.

Monroe, Myles, *The Burden of Freedom: Discover the Keys to Your Individual and National Freedom*, Charisma House, A Strang House, Publisher, Lake Mary, Florida, 2000, 2001.

Niebuhr, Reinhold, *Man and Immoral Society, A Study in Ethics and Politics*, Charles Scribner's Sons, Publisher, New York, 1932.

Odom, John Yancy, *Saving Black America: An Economic Plan For Civil Rights*, African American Images, Publisher, Chicago, Illinois, 2001.

Smiley, Tavis, Ed. Wright Edelman, "What We Can Do," *How to Make Black America Better: Leading African Americans Speak Out*, New York: Doubleday, 2001.

Thurman, Howard, *The Luminous Darkness*, Richmond, IN, Friends United Press, 1989.

Washington, James Melvin, Editor, Martin Luther King, Jr., *A Testament of Hope: The Essential Writings of Martin Luther King, Jr.*, Harper & Row, Publishers, San Francisco, 1986.

Watkins, Boyce, *Black American Money, How Black Power Can Thrive in a Capitalist Society*, Blue Boy Publishing Co., Camille's, NY, 2009.

————. *How To Think Like A Millionaire*, CreateSpace Independent Publishing Platform, 2017.

West, Cornel, *Race Matters*, Vintage Books, New York, 1993.

————. Edited and introduced, *The Radical King*, Beacon Press, Boston, Massachusetts, 2015.

William, Chancellor, *The Destruction of Black Civilization: Great Issues Of A Race From 4500 B.C. To 2000 A.D.*, BN Publishing, Hawthorne, California, 2012.

Wilson, Amos N., *The Blueprint For Black Power, A Moral, Political, and Economic Imperative for the Twenty-First Century*, Afrikan World InfoSystem, Publisher, Brooklyn, New York, 1998.

————. *The Falsification of AfriKan Consciousness*, African World InfoSystems, Publisher, Brooklyn, New York, 1993.

————. *The Developmental Psychology of The Black Child*, Africana Research Publication, New York, New York, 1978.

Woodson, Carter G., *The Miseducation of the Negro*, Africa World Press, Inc., Trenton, N.J., 1933.

Wright, Jr Jeremiah A., *What Makes You So Strong, Sermons of Joy and Strength*, Judson Press, Valley Forge, PA, 1993.

Articles

Littlejohn-Blake, Sheila M., and Carol Anderson Darling. "Understanding the Strengths of African American Families." *Journal of Black Studies*, vol. 23, no. 4, Sage Publications, Inc., 1993, pp. 460–71, http://www.jstor.org/stable/2784380.

Cassidy Dyce, "Why Martin Luther King, Jr.'s Quotes About Nonviolence Are Relevant," BorgenProject.org, March 27, 2018.

William R. Jones, Unpublished Lecture, "The Arts In The Community: Toward A Deeper Understanding of Black Aesthetics," *Religious and Philosophical Consideration*, 9-10.

Gary A. Johnson, "How Do Black People Spend Their Money?—The Racial Wealth Gap" by Black Men In America.com, June 30, 2021.

Stan Choe, AP Business Writer, ABC News, "Stocks Are Soaring, And Most Black People Are Missing Out," October 12, 2020.

J.D. Smith, "AFRICAN AMERICAN WEALTH MAY FALL TO ZERO BY 2053" by Charlene Rhinehart, *Black Enterprise*, July 12, 2019.

Erik Sherman, Senior Contributor of *Forbes*, "Median Wealth Of Black And Latino Families Could Hit Zero By The Middle Of The Century," September 11, 2017.

Sarah Keenan, "Elephants, Fathers, and Families," *Church Magazines*, The Church of Jesus Christ of Latter-day Saints, September 9, 2018.

Michael Lafitte, "Dads on Duty: Louisiana, fathers fan out at school to prevent violence, mentor kids," Makenzie Bouncher, *Shreveport Times*, October 30, 2021, USAtoday.com.

Teresa McCarthy, "Sticks And Stones: The Healing And Destructive Force of Language, An Exploration of the Theology of Language," Biola University, Center for Christian Thought, January 15, 2018.

Matthew Kondrat, "Does Culture Affect Music or Does Music Affect Culture?" June 16, 2014, Prezioso.com

Belinda Huang, "What Kind of Impact Does Our Music Really Make on Society?" August 24, 2015, blog.sonicbids.com.

Mislan, C. (2013). An "Obedient Servant." Journalism History, 39(2), 115–125.

Speeches

Mahatma Gandhi, Statement Before Mr. C.N. Broomfield, I.C.S., District and Sessions Judge, Ahmedabad, 18 March 1922

Malcolm X, "The Ballot or the Bullet," speech delivered in Detroit on April 12, 1964.

Martin Luther King, Jr., "I Have Been To the Mountain Top" Speech, Memphis, Tennessee, April 3, 1968.

Willie Lynch Speech, Banks of the James River, 1712.

Online

Mahatma Gandhi, www.brainyquotes.com 134846

Madam C.J. Walker, AZ quotes.com

Stephanie Lahart, "Black Wealth Quotes," Goodreads.com

Maya Angelou, *Still I Rise*, Poetry Foundation

Amanda Gordon, "*New Day's Lyric*," 2022, Instagram.com.

Dr. Da'Mond Holt, interviewed by Mansa Musa, "The Reality of Black Historical Trauma Making Healing A Form of Justice," June 3, 2024, https://therealnews.com.

ABOUT THE AUTHOR

Reginald F. Davis is a pastor, scholar, and native of Memphis, Tennessee. He is the author of eleven additional books in the field of theology and religion including *Depart From Me, The Dreadful Words of Jesus Christ to Many, A Theological Assessment of American Christianity and The Call for Unity to Solve Our National Problems Together, We Need Each Other to Transform America*. He has lectured at colleges, universities, and churches across the nation. He holds a Bachelor of Arts from Incarnate Word College, a Masters of Divinity from Colgate Rochester Divinity School, and a Ph.D. from Florida State University.

He lives in Williamsburg, Virginia, with his wife and children.

www.ingramcontent.com/pod-product-compliance
Lightning Source LLC
Chambersburg PA
CBHW012257240726
48656CB00007B/2421